PEOPLE OF THE BOOK

CRAIG CONSIDINE

People of the Book

*Prophet Muhammad's Encounters
with Christians*

HURST & COMPANY, LONDON

First published in the United Kingdom in 2021 by
C. Hurst & Co. (Publishers) Ltd.,
41 Great Russell Street, London, WC1B 3PL
© Craig Considine, 2021
All rights reserved.

The right of Craig Considine to be identified as the author
of this publication is asserted by him in accordance with the
Copyright, Designs and Patents Act, 1988.

Distributed in the United States, Canada and Latin America
by Oxford University Press, 198 Madison Avenue, New York,
NY 10016, United States of America.

A Cataloguing-in-Publication data record for this book
is available from the British Library.

ISBN: 9781787384712

This book is printed using paper from registered sustainable
and managed sources.

Printed and bound in Great Britain by Bell & Bain Ltd, Glasgow

www.hurstpublishers.com

To His Holiness Pope Francis, for helping me reimagine my faith, and for serving as a bridge between Christians and Muslims.

Blessed are the peacemakers, for they will be called the children of God.

– Matthew 5:9.

We have not sent you (O Muhammad) but as an unequaled mercy for all the worlds.

– Qur'an 21:107.

CONTENTS

ACKNOWLEDGMENTS

I owe a debt of gratitude to several scholars whose works gave me direction and knowledge in designing this book, my seventh. Mustafa Akyol's *The Islamic Jesus: How the King of the Jews Became a Prophet of the Muslims* (2017) provided insight into the dynamics of the early Christian Church and the sects of Christianity that arose out of Jerusalem in the first century. Several of Karen Armstrong's books on Muhammad's life and legacy offered rich perspectives on his vision for the *Ummah*, including *Muhammad: A Biography of the Prophet* (1993) and *Muhammad: A Prophet of Our Time* (2006). Historian Juan Cole's *Muhammad: Prophet of Peace amid the Clash of Empires* (2018) supplied a unique glimpse into Muhammad's encounters with Christians, particularly in those associated with the Byzantine Empire. Fred M. Donner's *Muhammad and the Believers: At the Origins of Islam* (2010) served as a key resource in understanding the inclusive nature of the early Islamic community in relation to the Believers as the People of the Book. The seminal *Muhammad: His Life Based on the Earliest Sources* (2006) by Martin Lings contributed invaluable material on the details of Muhammad's actions and the trajectory of his life. Finally, Garry Wills's *What the Qur'an Meant and Why It Matters* (2017) gave me plenty of inspiration in terms of engaging with the Islamic tradition as a Christian and academic aiming to write both an accessible and scholarly book.

LIST OF ILLUSTRATIONS

1. "The Ancient City of Busra, Syria." Courtesy Valdemar Bednarz, via Wikimedia Commons, Attribution-ShareAlike 4.0 International (CC BY-SA 4.0).
2. "Camel Caravan to Mecca, 1910." Courtesy American Colony (Jerusalem), via Library of Congress.
3. "The Holy Ka'bah." Courtesy Richard Mortel, via Wikimedia Commons, Attribution 2.0 Generic (CC BY 2.0).
4. "Syriac Orthodox Monastery of Saint Matthew Overlooking the Nineveh Plain." Courtesy Levy Clancy, via Wikimedia Commons, Attribution-ShareAlike 4.0 International (CC BY-SA 4.0).
5. "The Angel Gabriel." Dated between 1308 and 1311. Courtesy Duccio Di Buoninsegna, Collection Du Huis Bergh, via Wikimedia Commons.
6. "Ethiopia-Axum Cathedral—Fresco—Black Madonna." A fresco of a black Madonna and Jesus at the Church of Our Lady Mary of Zion in Axum, Ethiopia. Courtesy Miko Stavrev, via Wikimedia Commons, Attribution 3.0 Unported (CC BY 3.0).
7. "Jerusalem, 2013, Temple Mount Dome of the Rock & Chain." The Dome of the Chain in front of the Dome of the Rock on the Temple Mount in the Old City of Jerusalem.

Map of the Near East in 570

GLOSSARY

ahadith/hadith	The Arabic words *ahadith* (plural) and *hadith* (singular) relate to the actions, advice, recommendations, and sayings of Muhammad, the prophet of Islam.
Ahl al-Kitab	The Arabic word that translates as "The People of the Book." The Qur'an refers to Jews, Christians, and Sabians as Ahl al-Kitab who had been given divine books before God revealed the Islamic sacred text to Muhammad starting in 610.
Ahl al-Suffah	The Arabic phrase that translates to, "The People of the Bench," a group named after the people that congregated at a stone bench near the colonnade of al-Masjid al-Nabawi. The People of the Bench were mostly farmers or tradesmen, such as Salman al-Farisiy.
al-Ansar	The Arabic word that translates to "the Helpers," the title Muhammad gave to the local inhabitants of Medina who welcomed him and his followers after they had migrated from Mecca in 615.

al-Ameen
: The Arabic word that translates to "the Trusted One," the nickname that the Meccans gave to Muhammad when he was a boy. Muhammad's nickname stayed with him into adulthood owing to his reputation as a trustworthy merchant.

al-Habib
: The Arabic word that translates to "the Beloved," the phrase a person may use when speaking about a close friend or family member.

Al-Lat
: The Arabic word that refers to the pre-Islamic goddess worshipped around the Arabian Peninsula; worshipped in Mecca alongside Al-'Uzza and Manat.

Al-Masih
: The Arabic name that translates to "The Messiah." The Messiah is a reference to Jesus.

Al-Madina al-Munawwarah
: The Arabic phrase that translates to "The Enlightened City," the name that replaced Yathrib as the official name of the ancient city and location of the second migration.

al-Mu'minun
: The Arabic term that translates to "the Believers"; generally refers to Muslims specifically but also extends to other monotheistic believers in Muhammad's prophethood.

Al-Quds
: The Arabic name for Jerusalem that translates to "The Holy One."

Al-'Uzza
: The Arabic word that refers to the pre-Islamic goddess worshipped around the Arabian Peninsula; worshipped in Mecca alongside Al-Lat and Manat.

al-Sadiq	The Arabic word that translates to "the Truthful one."
Allah	The Arabic word that translates to "God."
'Allahu 'akbar	The Arabic word that translates to "God is Most Great," the phrase used by Muslims in prayers and as a general declaration of faith.
'amir	The Arabic word that refers to "king" or an aristocratic noble.
an-saab	The Arabic word that translates to "idols," the statues worshipped by pagans in the pre-Islamic period.
'aqib	The Arabic word that translates to "final"; it is also a nickname given to Muhammad as the final prophet of the monotheistic tradition as noted in the Qur'an.
Ar-Rum	The Arabic word that translates to "The Romans," the name the Qur'an uses to refer to the Byzantines or the Greeks; also the name of the thirtieth chapter of the Qur'an.
as-salamu 'alaykum	The Arabic greeting that translates to "peace be unto you."
'asabiyya	The Arabic word that translates to "social cohesion" through solidarity across cultural, ethnic, and religious lines; first developed by Ibn Khaldun in *Muqaddimah* (1377).
Augustus/Augusti	The Latin word that translates to "majestic," the title given to Roman emperors.
azzan	The Arabic term that refers to the Islamic call to prayer.
badawah	The Arabic term that refers to the

"nomadic" lifestyle found on the Arabian Peninsula.

bar nasha The Aramaic term that translates to "son of man."

bizuah The Hebrew term that translates to "mediation."

khalifah The Arabic term that refers to the "supreme Muslim head of state" who governs over the *Ummah*, or "nation."

Christianismi restitutio The Latin title for "The Restoration of Christianity," the title of a book published in 1553 by Michael Servetus, a Christian who rejected the doctrine of the Trinity.

Corpus juris civilis The Latin phrase that translates to "Body of Civil Law," the order issued by Justinian I, the Byzantine emperor.

dimmi The Islamic concept that refers to "protected person"; generally refers to non-Muslim groups living in Muslim-majority countries or nations governed by Islamic legal precepts.

Domus Sanctae Marthae The Latin name for "Saint Martha's House," a building adjacent to Saint Peter's Basilica in Vatican City.

ebyonim The Hebrew word that means "the poor" or "poor ones." The Ebionites are followers of the Jewish Christian sect of early Christianity.

gazu The Arabic term that refers to the acquisition raids on trading caravans carried out by clans and tribes.

Ghar Sawr The Arabic name given to the "Cave of Sawr," in which Muhammad took refuge

	from the Quraysh on his way to Medina during the first migration of 622.
gnosis	The Greek word for "knowledge." *Gnostikos* is a derivative of *gnosis*, which translates to "good at knowing."
hajj	The Arabic word that means "to attend a journey." In Islamic terminology, it refers to the Muslim pilgrimage to Mecca. All Muslims are expected to make at least one pilgrimage once in their lifetime.
halakha	The Hebrew term that translates to "to walk to" or "to go to"; more broadly, it refers to Jewish law as interpreted through rabbinic legal texts.
hamada	The Arabic term that translates to mean "highly praised"; a nickname of Muhammad.
hanif/hunafa'	The Arabic word that translates to "true believer." In pre-Islamic times, a *hanif* is a person who maintained the monotheistic faith of Abraham.
Harun	The Arabic name for Aaron, the Islamic prophet, high priest of the Hebrews, and the older brother of Moses, the biblical prophet.
hijra	The Arabic term that refers to "migration." The first *hijra* occurred around 615 when the Believers traveled to the Christian kingdom of Abyssinia. The second *hijra* unfolded around 622 when the Believers traveled to Yathrib, which later became Medina.

Idris — The Arabic term that translates to "interpreter." According to the Islamic tradition, it is also the name for Enoch, the third prophet mentioned in the Bible.

ijtihad — The Arabic term referring to "independent reasoning."

'Isa — The Arabic name for Jesus, who is referred to as the son of Mary in the Qur'an, and the Son of God for Christians.

islam — The Arabic term that refers to one's "submission" to the Will of God in order to achieve peace.

Isra — The Arabic word that translates to "Journey of the Night." Its meaning refers to Muhammad's night journey to Jerusalem with Buraq, the supernatural animal, and Angel Gabriel.

iqra — The Arabic word that translates to "read." It is also a root of the word *qur'an*, which means "recitation."

istislah — The Arabic word that means "to deem proper." In Islamic law, or *shari'ah*, it is used by jurists to solve problems that do not have clear answers according to the Qur'an.

Jabal an-Nur — The Arabic words that translate to "Mountain of Light." Located near Mecca, it is the site where Muhammad is said to have received the first revelations from God in 610.

Jabal Thawr — The Arabic words that translate to "Mount Bull." Located near Mecca, it is the site where Muhammad and Abu

	Bakr, his companion, hid in a cave for three days before migrating to Medina in 622.
jahiliyah	The Arabic word that translates to "ignorance." An Islamic term referring to the period of time before Muhammad started receiving revelations from God in 610.
jinn	The Arabic word that refers to "evil spirits" or "demonic creatures" who do harm to people.
jizya	The Arabic word that historically relates to the tax paid by non-Muslim populations to their Muslim rulers.
kafir	The Arabic word that translates to "disbeliever" or "infidel." Used to refer to people who reject Muhammad's messages and Islamic teachings.
Laylat al-Qadr	The Arabic phrase that refers to "The Night of Destiny" in which Muhammad encountered Angel Gabriel in the cave at Mount Hira. The encounter begins the revelation of the Qur'an, the Islamic holy text.
masjid	The Arabic word for "mosque," a place of worship for followers of the Islamic faith.
Al-Masjid al-Dirar	The Arabic phrase for "The Mosque of Dissent." Muhammad destroyed the mosque following the Expedition of Tabuk.
Al-Masjid al-Haram	The Arabic phrase for "The Forbidden Mosque." Located in Mecca, it surrounds al-Kaʿbah.

GLOSSARY

Al-Masjid al-Nabawi	The Arabic phrase for "The Prophet's Mosque." Located in Medina, it was the third mosque built in Islamic history.
Mi'raj	The Arabic word that means "ascension."
mubahala	The Arabic term and Islamic concept that means "invocation of God's curse;" mentioned in the early Islamic sources in reference to Muhammad's encounter with the Christians of Najran in Medina.
Muqaddimah	The Arabic word that refers to "Introduction," and a book published by Ibn Khaldun in 1377.
Najashi	The Arabic term that translates to "Ruler" and refers to Ashama Ibn Abjar, the Christian king of Abyssinia who protected the Believers during the first migration.
namus	The Arabic term that translates to "law."
Negus	The Ethiopian title for "King" in early Islamic sources, refers to Ashama Ibn Abjar, the Christian king of the Abyssinian Empire who hosted and sheltered the Believers during the first *hijra* of 615.
Patrologia Graeca	The Latin title of a book published by Jacques Paul Mignes, a French priest, between 1857 and 1866. The book is a collection of edited writings (written in Greek) that is regarded as the largest ever published collection of Christian and secular writings of the early and medieval Christian church.
p'sharah	The Hebrew term that translates to "arbitration."

Peshitta   The Syriac word that translates to "common" or "simple." The name Peshitta is also the name given to the Syriac version of the Bible that was first accepted by Syrian churches at the end of the third century.

qiblah   The Arabic word that refers to the direction that Muslims should face when praying.

qur'an   The Arabic term that translates to "recitation" and refers to the Islamic holy text that was revealed to Muhammad over the span of twenty-two years (from 610 to 632).

riba   The Islamic concept (in the Arabic language) that refers to "usury" or "charged interest" in Islamic banking.

ruh   The Arabic term and Islamic concept that refers to a person's "soul" or "spirit."

shari'ah   The Arabic term that translates to "path" or the "path to the watering hole"; also referred to in light of "Islamic law."

as-shahada   The Arabic term referring to the declaration of the Islamic faith, which reads: "I bear witness that there is no deity but God, and I bear witness that Muhammad is the messenger of God."

silm   The Arabic term that translates to "to feel peace."

sira   The Arabic term that translates to "life" or "life journey."

Sunnah   The Arabic term that refers to traditional Islamic customs and practice in both the social and legal realms of society.

surah	The Arabic term that translates to "chapter" of the Qur'an.
Surah Maryam	The Arabic phrase that translates to "Chapter of Mary." It is the nineteenth chapter of the Qur'an and consists of ninety-eight verses.
Surah al-Zumar	The Arabic phrase that translates to "Chapter of the Troops." It is the thirty-ninth chapter of the Qur'an and consists of seventy-five verses.
Tariqah	The Islamic concept and Arabic term that refers to the Sufi way of life and learning.
tawhid	The Arabic word that translates to "oneness." It is also an Islamic phrase that relates to the notion of the oneness of God.
Ummah	The Arabic word that translates to "community" or "nation."
'Umrah	The Arabic word that refers to "visiting a populated place"; refers to the "Lesser Pilgrimage" to Mecca.
Yusuf	The Arabic name for "Joseph."
zakat	The Arabic term for "charity."

CHRONOLOGY

36 According to the New Testament (Galatians 1:17), Paul the Apostle begins his ministry by spending three years in Arabia. It is likely that Paul spent time in Petra, a city of the Nabatean kingdom on the eastern side of Transjordan.

62 The Epistle of James, a book in the New Testament, is written by James the Just, believed to be the brother of Jesus, who served as the leader of the Jerusalem Church. James is said to have believed in a stricter form of monotheism than Paul the Apostle, who expressed the Trinitarian belief of the Father, the Son, and the Holy Spirit.

70 The Siege of Jerusalem takes place four years after the start of the Jewish revolt in Jerusalem in 66. The Roman Empire destroys the Temple of Solomon. A large Jewish diaspora begins. The Christians of Jerusalem fled and dispersed throughout the Near East region.

206 Abgar V, the king of Osroene, also referred to as Ukkama in the Syriac dialect, converts to Christianity. He is believed to have been one of the first kings in history to convert to Christianity.

270 Saint Anthony the Great, a Christian monk, begins his monastic movement in the Eastern Desert of Egypt. Athanasius of Alexandria, Anthony's biographer, helped to spread the concept of monasticism throughout the world.

311 The Edict of Galerius is issued by Emperor Galerius of the Roman Empire. The edict granted the Christians of the Roman Empire the freedom to privately practice Christianity, a right they had not been previously granted by the emperors of Rome.

312 Emperor Constantine, a pagan, has a vision at the Battle of the Milvian Bridge near Rome of a cross while gazing into the sun. The cross had the words "by this sign, you shall conquer" on it. Constantine's victory at the Milvian Bridge paves the way for the official adoption of Christianity as the state religion of the Roman Empire, which would later be reconceived as the Byzantine Empire, with its capital in Constantinople, or the "City of Constantine."

313 The Edict of Milan is issued by Emperors Constantine and Licinius of the Roman Empire. The edict permanently established the toleration of Christianity within the Roman Empire by granting freedom of religion, assuring legal rights, and directing the return of previously seized properties of Christian populations.

324 King Ezana II converts to Christianity through the influence of Frumentius, the founder of the Church of Abyssinia, which later emerges as the center of the Abyssinian Empire in the northeastern region of Africa.

325 The Council of Nicaea is ordered by Emperor Constantine of the Roman Empire. The ecumenical council was the first attempt by Christian bishops to reach a consensus on the nature of Jesus. The council's final ruling deemed Jesus to be the Son of God, thus making him divine. The Nicene Creed, which established the Christian doctrine known as the Trinity, was also included as part of the council's final ruling.

326 Helena, the mother of Emperor Constantine, discovers the True Cross, or Holy Cross, on which Jesus was reportedly crucified, in Jerusalem.

381 The Council of Constantinople is ordered by Emperor Theodosius in Constantinople. The council further developed the Nicene Creed by declaring that the Holy Spirit, a component of the Trinity, is equal to the Father and the Son, the other two elements of Trinitarianism. The Council of Constantinople also affected internal group dynamics among Christians by making Constantinople the "New Rome," or the center of Christendom.

391 In Damascus, Emperor Theodosius of the Byzantine Empire converts the Temple of Jupiter, constructed by Emperor Augustus of the Roman Empire, into a cathedral, thus formally introducing Christianity to the Syrians.

428 Nestorius, a Christian theologian and the archbishop of Constantinople, starts preaching that Mary (Jesus's mother) is *Christokos* (the Birth-Giver of Christ) rather than *Theotokos* (the Birth-Giver of God). In other words, Nestorius argues that Jesus is at least partially human.

431 The Council of Ephesus is held at the Church of Mary in Ephesus, Anatolia, in an effort to either confirm or refute the teachings of Nestorius, who claimed that Mary is *Christokos*. The council confirmed the Nicene Creed and condemned Nestorius as a heretic.

451 The Council of Chalcedon is called by Emperor Marcian to condemn Monophysitism, a sect of Christianity developed primarily by Eutyches. The council concluded that Jesus has two natures (Godhood and manhood) in one person and hypostasis.

490 Hashim, Muhammad's great-grandfather, is said to have visited Christian leaders of the Byzantine Empire in Damascus to negotiate tariff reductions and safe travel passages for Meccan trading caravans journeying into Byzantine territories.

570 Muhammad, whose full name is Muhammad ibn ʿAbdullah,

is born in Mecca, a city known as a center of trade and polytheistic worship. Muhammad's name derives from *hamada*, the Arabic word that means "highly praised," "to praise," or "to glorify." He is born to Abd Allah bin al-Muttalib (d. 570), his father, who died before Muhammad was born. Muhammad's male ancestors were part of the Hashim clan of the Qurayshite tribe. Muhammad's mother, Amina bint Wahb (d. 578), placed the fatherless Muhammad under the care of Halima, a nurse from the Bedouin tribe of Sa'id ibn Bakr. Bint Wahb's decision was in keeping with Meccan traditions for widows.

574   Halima bint Abu Dhuayb brings Muhammad to Amina, his mother, who was then living in Mecca. A year later, Amina dies on her journey from Yathrib (later renamed Medina) to Mecca while bringing Muhammad to visit his father's grave. Now an orphan, Muhammad is placed under the care of Abdul al-Muttalib, his paternal grandfather, who was living in Mecca.

582   Now around twelve years old, Muhammad travels with Abu Talib, his uncle and guardian, on a trading caravan to Syria. Muhammad interacts with Bahira, a Christian monk, who predicts Muhammad's forthcoming prophethood.

590   'Uthman Ibn al-Huwayritah, a monotheist and member of the Quraysh tribe living in Mecca, travels to Constantinople, the capital of the Byzantine Empire, where he is reported to have asked its Christian leaders if they would assist him in his effort to rise to power as the sole ruler of Mecca.

595   Muhammad, a merchant responsible for guiding trading caravans, marries his boss Khadijah bint Khuwaylid, a forty-year-old widow and wealthy businesswoman. On one caravan excursion, Muhammad is reported to have encountered Nestor, a Christian monk. Muhammad and Khadijah had six children together—four daughters and two sons, both of whom passed away in infancy.

603　Muhammad, now in his early thirties, learns about the Persian Empire's invasion of Byzantium in the Near East. The invasion marked the beginning of twenty-six years of warfare between the Byzantines and Persians.

605　The Qurayshite leaders rebuild al-Ka'bah, the holy sanctuary in Mecca that had fallen into disrepair. Al-Ka'bah holds the celestial black stone that is reported to have been brought to Abraham by an angel from Abu Qubays, a nearby hill. The Quraysh are said to have gathered wood from the ship of a Christian merchant which had been wrecked near Jeddah. A Copt is reported to have used his carpentry skills to build al-Ka'bah's roof.

610　Muhammad withdraws to a cave on Mount Hira, where he receives the first revelations of the Qur'an, the Islamic holy text, from Angel Gabriel. Muhammad then returns to Mecca and shares his experience with Khadijah, his wife, who believed in the authenticity of the revelations. Khadijah, as such, becomes the first Believer in Muhammad's message. Muhammad also meets Waraqa Ibn Nawfal, a Christian who also recognized the legitimacy of Muhammad's experience on Mount Hira. Zaid, a young boy and reportedly a Christian, also embraces the Islamic faith in this year.

613　Muhammad starts to publicly preach the form of monotheism that became known as Islam in Mecca.

614　Shahrbaraz, a general of the Persian Empire, conquers Jerusalem. Shahrbaraz massacres thousands of Christians, burns churches, and captures Zachariah, the leader of the Jerusalem Church. The Persian general also steals the True Cross.

615　A small group of Believers escapes persecution in Mecca by migrating across the Red Sea to Abyssinia, a Christian kingdom in northeast Africa. A second wave of Believers follows soon thereafter. This migratory event is popularly referred to as the first *hijra*. The *Negus*, or King of Abyssinia, is Ashama Ibn Abjar, who hosts and shelters the Believers. He discusses a range of topics with them including the nature of both Jesus and Mary. King Ibn Abjar refuses to hand over the Believers to their enemies, the Qurayshites of Mecca, who ask the *Negus* to extradite them to Mecca to face charges.

617   A feud between the Aws and Khazraj, two tribes of the city of Yathrib, breaks out into an all-out war referred to as the Battle of Bu'ath, the last major violent conflict among the Yathribite tribes before Muhammad's arrival in 622.

619   Abu Talib, Muhammad's uncle, and Khadijah, his first wife, pass away in the "Year of Sorrow." Although he had never identified himself as a Believer or Muslim, Abu Talib had consistently defended Muhammad and the early Believers against their Qurayshite enemies until his death.

621   Angel Gabriel and Buraq, a supernatural animal, fly Muhammad from Mecca to Jerusalem in what is generally known as the "Night Journey to Jerusalem." The first part of the story, known as Isra, brings Muhammad to the Temple of Solomon. In the second part of the story, known as the Mi'raj, Muhammad reaches the Seven Stages of Heaven and meets Abraham, Jesus, and Moses, among other monotheistic prophets.

622   Muhammad and several hundred of his followers flee persecution in Mecca by migrating northward to the town of Yathrib, which the Believers later rename Medina, where Muhammad establishes a civic-oriented community consisting of the Believers, the Helpers (al-Ansar), Jewish tribes, and possibly even Christians. The civic-oriented community was rooted in a legal and political framework known as the Constitution of Medina.

624   A new revelation is given to Muhammad that commands the Believers to turn their bodies toward al-Ka'bah when

engaging in prayer. The Believers had previously been turning their bodies toward Jerusalem.

627 Ibn Jahsh, a Christian cousin of Muhammad, dies in Abyssinia. He had fled Mecca during the first *hijra* but later reconverted to Christianity in Axum.

628 The Treaty of Hudaybiyyah is agreed upon by Muhammad and the Qurayshite leaders. The agreement declares a ten-year truce between the Believers and the Qurayshites. Part of the Treaty of Hudaybiyyah allows Muhammad and his followers to enter Mecca to visit al-Ka'bah in 629.

629 The Battle of Mu'tah takes place between the Byzantines and the Believers east of the Jordan River and close to the city of Karak. The battle breaks out after one of Muhammad's emissaries was murdered while delivering a letter to a Byzantine ally in the city of Busra. Muhammad also marries Maria, the Copt from Egypt, and the Believers engage in the *'Umrah*.

630 Muhammad and the Believers triumphantly return to Mecca in a "peaceful conquest." The Qurayshites, who had persecuted and fought the Believers for many years, surrender the city to Muhammad. Muhammad rids al-Ka'bah of its idols, paintings, pictures, and statues but reportedly preserves a painting of Jesus and Mary as a sign of respect and reverence.

632 Muhammad gives the Farewell Sermon on Mount Arafat, near Mecca. Soon thereafter, he passes away and one day later is buried in Medina.

INTRODUCTION

I am inspired by the Qur'an's inclusion of Christians and Jews as Ahl al-Kitab, the Arabic term that translates to "The People of the Book."[1] The pluralistic nature of the term is evident in the use of the noun "book" in the singular tense rather than the plural form. The phrasing emphasizes the notion that Jews, Christians, and Muslims follow, in essence, one and the same book, and not conflicting scriptures.[2]

I wrote this book as a Christian who is also inspired by the "culture of encounter," especially as it pertains to fostering stronger relations between Christians and Muslims. His Holiness Pope Francis described the culture of encounter in a 2016 morning meditation in the Chapel of Domus Sanctae Marthae near Saint Peter's Basilica in Vatican City, in which he encouraged Christians to follow Jesus by "not just seeing, but looking; not just hearing, but listening, not just passing people by, but stopping with them … [by being moved] with compassion."[3] Pope Francis called on Christians to engage in a deeper, fearless, and more authentic kind of encounter with the Other. "Faith is an encounter with Jesus," he said, "and we must do what Jesus does: encounter others."

His Holiness and Grand Imam Ahmad Al-Tayyeb of Al-'Azhar University have paved the way for a culture of encounter between Christians and Muslims, a culture that is at the heart of

1

Muhammad's encounters with the Christians of his time. Together, the pope and grand imam authored and signed "A Document on Human Fraternity for World Peace and Living Together," which reads:

> Al-'Azhar al-Sharif and the Muslims of the East and West, together with the Catholic Church and the Catholics of the East and West, declare the adoption of a culture of dialogue as the path; mutual cooperation as the code of conduct; reciprocal understanding as the method and standard.

> We, who believe in God and in the final meeting with Him and His judgment, on the basis of our religious and moral responsibility, and through this Document, call upon ourselves, upon the leaders of the world as well as the architects of international policy and world economy, to work strenuously to spread the culture of tolerance and of living together in peace; to intervene at the earliest opportunity to stop the shedding of innocent blood and bring an end to wars, conflicts, environmental decay and the moral and cultural decline that the world is presently experiencing.

Pope Francis and Imam Al-Tayyeb remind Christians and Muslims that they are part of the same monotheistic tradition, and that both populations are challenged with the task of peace-making, and not merely peacekeeping. Peacekeepers, while important for the sake of maintaining safety and stability in our communities, are oftentimes maintaining the status quo. Peacemakers, on the other hand, are actively engaged in ushering in changes that are necessary to promote cooperation, dialogue, peace, and understanding across the perceived religious divides. This book explores Muhammad's actions of peacemaking but does not shy away from the moments when he had to forcefully engage with the Christians around the Arabian Peninsula.

As a US citizen, I am also inspired by Muhammad's vision of establishing a civic nation that is rooted in egalitarian values and the democratic rule of law. My understanding of the *Ummah*, or

INTRODUCTION

"Muslim nation," as a civic nation arose after learning about a decision made by Franklin Delano Roosevelt (d. 1945), the thirty-second president of the United States, in 1931. President Roosevelt chose Adolph A. Weinman, an accomplished sculptor, to carve a marble frieze in the US Supreme Court building. Roosevelt asked Weinman to create a frieze that would symbolize US national identity. Weinman decided to depict the sixteen greatest lawgivers in the history of the world.[4]

Weinman, you may have guessed it, included Muhammad as one of the greatest lawgivers to have ever lived.[5]

My goal with this book is to shed light on how Muhammad and the Believers of the early *Ummah* created a nation founded upon allyship, civility, cross-cultural interactions, freedom of conscience, freedom of religion, freedom of speech, interreligious dialogue, mutual dependency, and religious pluralism. While clashes between Christians and Muslims may have erupted sporadically in Muhammad's lifetime, they were the exception to the norm.

Another goal of this book is to shed light on the Christians living in Muhammad's midst. The Christians around the Arabian Peninsula during his lifetime have been largely overlooked, despite being one of the oldest Christian communities in the world. According to Galatians 1:17–24, Paul the Apostle (d. 67), also known as Saint Paul or simply Paul, is the first Christian to have traveled to the Arabian Peninsula, where he is thought to have preached for about three years.[6] Paul used the term "Arabia" to refer to the ethnically Arab and Aramaic-speaking people of the Nabataean kingdom that he had encountered when visiting Petra. The Nabataean kingdom encompassed an area that stretched as far north as Damascus and as far south as northwestern Arabia, a region known as the Hijaz.

As Paul traveled throughout Arabia, he is believed to have developed his own theology outside of the Jerusalem Church, which was reportedly led by James (d. 69), one of the original twelve Disciples and the brother (or perhaps the step-brother) of Jesus. While James is said to have taught a rigid monotheism, with God (and not Jesus) as the ultimate divine source, Paul was teaching the Trinity, the theological position in which God (the Father), his Son (Jesus), and the Holy Spirit reflected the true nature and Will of God.

These Christological differences had a significant impact on Muhammad's encounters with the Christians of his time. Muhammad not only entered into treaties with these Christians but he also befriended them—and was inspired by them—on many occasions. This book explores these dynamics.

While some scholars dispute the authenticity and credibility of Muhammad's reported encounters with Christians, I am in agreement with Hugh Goddard, who states that "there seems to be no good reason to discount the accounts."[7] I also agree with Omid Safi, who claims that Muhammad's encounters with Christians "happened, and indeed, there is no reason to suspect that they did not."[8]

I have structured the book into six chapters that follow Muhammad's encounters with Christians in chronological order. Chapter 1 ("Monks and Merchants") examines his interaction with the monk Bahira in 582 and explains his experiences as a cross-cultural navigator while working as a merchant around the Arabian Peninsula. Chapter 2 ("Angels and Mystics") dives into his encounter with the Angel Gabriel on the Night of Destiny in 615 and considers the origins of the Believers movement. Chapter 3 ("Allies and Prophets") explains the persecution experienced by the Believers, turns to the allyship displayed by the Christians of Abyssinia during the first migration in 615, and surveys the significance of the Night Journey to Jerusalem around 621. Chapter 4 ("Citizens and Rebels") reviews the civic nation, developed through the Constitution of Medina during the second migration of the Believers in 622, while also setting the stage for Muhammad's future encounters with the Byzantine Empire. Chapter 5 ("Guests and Hosts") explores his encounter with the Christians of Najran and how their meeting with Muhammad at al-Masjid al-Nabawi in 630 ushered in a pluralist vision of society for the Arabian Peninsula. Chapter 6 ("Symbols and Souls") covers Muhammad's peaceful return to Mecca in 630, the rededication of al-Ka'bah, his last encounters with Christians, and finally the Farewell Sermon in 632.

Let me also alert readers to the valuable knowledge provided in the endnotes of this book. As you read through the chapters, be sure to consider reading the endnotes for further insight into Muhammad's encounters with Christians, the Christians living around the Arabian Peninsula from the first to the seventh centuries, the theological differences and similarities between Christianity and Islam, and other valuable contemporary and historical information that will inform your understanding of the People of the Book.

While my aim is to be as objective as possible, I am mindful of my position as an Islamic apologist who is concerned with the state of relations between Christians and Muslims. Although some scholars are skeptical about the methodology of apologetics, other scholars, like Paul J. Griffiths, see it as a vital component of effective efforts in interreligious dialogue.

Scholars should never truly divorce themselves from their own lived experiences. As Stuart Hall (d. 2014) put it: "You have to position yourself somewhere in order to say anything at all."[9]

1

MONKS AND MERCHANTS

Around the year 582, the twelve-year-old Muhammad (d. 632) traveled southward toward Busra with Abu Talib (d. 619), his uncle, as Meccan caravans usually did after trading in Syria. Busra was a walled city located about 90 miles to the south of Damascus.[1] The city was populated mainly by Christians and sprinkled with monasteries. Busra also had exquisite gates, a Byzantine imperial-styled arch, and a skyline marked by its domed cathedral.[2]

As the capital of Syria, a province of both the Roman Empire and the Byzantine Empire from the first to the sixth centuries, Busra was a center of Christianity in the Near East that served as the seat of the Byzantine governor as well as the seat of the archbishop of Busra. According to Ibn Ishaq, Muhammad's mother, Amina (d. 578), dreamt of Busra's castles while she was pregnant with Muhammad.[3] The castles may have been the monastic towers in which Christian ascetics and mystics lived.

In Busra, Abu Talib's caravan crossed, as the Meccan caravans typically did, the small dwelling cells of hermits and monks. On this particular occasion, his caravan encountered a monk named

Bahira, whose name is derived from the Syriac word *bhira*, which translates to "approved" or "tested" by God.[4] The twelve-year-old Muhammad was an orphan living under the protection of his uncle at this time in his life.[5] Al-Tirmidhi (d. 892) and various other historians have reported Muhammad's encounters with Bahira.[6]

On a typical day, Bahira would have likely paid little or no attention to the passing Meccan merchants. On this particular occasion, however, he is said to have had a "revelation" from God.

Bahira decided to stop the caravan to invite the Meccans into his cell. Abu Talib and his peers accepted the invitation, and upon leaving their camels and goods, the merchants left behind Muhammad. Leaving a child behind in this manner was a normal practice; a younger member of a trading caravan would typically watch over the caravan's property and hopefully keep it safe from *badawah* and *gazu* practices.[7]

While guarding the caravan, a small, low-hanging protective cloud remained stationary over the tree in which the young Muhammad and the caravan took shelter from the Syrian sun.[8] Perhaps Bahira interpreted the cloud hanging over Muhammad as the sign of the long-awaited prophet, as foretold by the Christian scriptures that he (and previous generations of monks) had read and studied in their small cells in Busra.[9]

Before the trading caravan left Bahira's cell in Busra, he asked Muhammad about Al-Lat and Al-'Uzza. Al-Lat, whose name is a derivative of al-Illahat, the Arabic term for "the Goddess," is thought to have been a similar goddess to Athena, the mother of all the gods in Greek polytheism. Al-'Uzza, the Arabic term for "the Strong One," was a widely venerated goddess among the Arab deities. She is said to have had a temple in Petra and may have been the city's patron goddess.

In response to Bahira's question about the gods, Muhammad is reported to have said: "Do not ask me about Al-Lat and Al-'Uzza, for by God, nothing is more hateful to me than these two."

Muhammad's clear rejection of polytheism was sufficient for Bahira, a monotheist himself.

After encountering Muhammad in person, Bahira felt that he might be a match for the physical description of the long-awaited prophet as foretold by the ancient texts handed down by Christian hermits and monks. He was particularly interested in seeing if the young boy had the sign of prophethood on his upper back.

It was between Muhammad's shoulders that Bahira found the "seal of prophethood." Bahira then told Abu Talib, Muhammad's guardian, to go back to Mecca with the boy and to keep him safe from emotional and physical harm. According to Islamic sources, Bahira was referring to Jewish people, who he predicted would do harm to Muhammad if they came to learn about his coming prophethood.[10]

As William Montgomery Watt has noted, this is of course only a story, but "it is significant because it expresses a popular Muslim view of Muhammad. He was a man who had been marked out from his early youth, even from before his birth, by supernatural signs and qualities."[11]

Who was Bahira?

Who was this Christian monk that reportedly predicted Muhammad's future prophethood? The *Patrologia Graeca* portrays Bahira as a renegade Christian heretic who was likely either an Arian or Jacobite.[12] John of Damascus (d. 749) also identified Bahira as an Arian, the term given to followers of Arianism, as conceived by Arius (d. 336), the North African presbyter from Alexandria, Egypt. The Arian teaching can be summarized as follows:

> [Jesus] was created out of nothing; hence, He is different in essence
> from the Father; that He is Logos, Wisdom, Son of God, is only of

9

grace. He is not so in himself. There was, when He was not; or, i.e., He is a finite being. He was created before everything else, and through Him the universe was created and is administered.[13]

Many of the Qur'anic accounts about God are similar to, or at least do not contradict, Arius's beliefs on the nature of the Almighty. The Qur'an, in fact, emphasizes that God is the sole Creator and that Jesus, like Abraham, Moses, and Muhammad, was a human prophet of God that should be praised, admired, and followed, but not worshiped as though he were God. While Arius believed that Jesus was divine, he also claimed that he was not equal to God, a claim that the Qur'an generally accepts to be true.[14]

Put another way, Bahira—like Arius before him—may have rejected the idea that Jesus was himself God.[15] Arius was eventually excommunicated from the Church in 321 and is said to have migrated to Asia Minor, where he converted many polytheists to Christianity. Arianism was later classified as a Christian heresy at the end of the Council of Nicaea (325), which Emperor Constantine (d. 337) of the Roman Empire had summoned to determine the "true nature" of Jesus.[16]

In meeting Bahira, Muhammad had likely encountered a Christian heretic, at least according to Byzantine leaders in Constantinople, whose views on Jesus's nature were neither mainstream nor popular. Bahira is believed to be the first human being to have recognized Muhammad as a future prophet of the Arab people, and indeed the world.

The cross-cultural navigator and husband

Muhammad likely had more encounters with Christians while he was traveling on the trading caravans in the early years of his life. In doing so, he followed in the footsteps of his Quraysh ancestors.[17] Muhammad's great-grandfather (Hashim ibn 'Abd

Manaf) and grandfather (Al-Muttalib ibn Hashim) were involved in the caravan trading network around the Arabian Peninsula. Together, the father and son participated in two specific annual journeys along the region's ancient incense routes—the Caravan of Winter to Yemen and the Caravan of Summer to Palestine and Syria. The latter two locations were ruled by Christian leaders under the authority of the Byzantine emperors. Yemen also reportedly had a small Christian population, particularly in Najran, a city located in the southwestern part of the Arabian Peninsula.

Muhammad grew up hearing stories about his ancestors' encounters with the Christians. Hashim, his great-grandfather, may have visited Byzantine authorities in Damascus around 490 to negotiate tariff reductions and safe traveling passages for Meccan merchants journeying into Byzantine territory, which stretched from Constantinople, across Asia Minor, down through Syria, and into Palestine and Egypt. Muhammad's ancestors, as Martin Lings (2006) points out, also likely had access to the goods of various Christian traders and craftsmen in Axum, the capital of Abyssinia, the Christian kingdom located across the Red Sea in northeast Africa that I explore in detail in Chapter 3.[18]

Muhammad's travels on the trading caravans of the Near East suggest that he would have been familiar with Byzantine law, culture, and languages, as well the customs and traditions of other Christian populations throughout the Near East. Juan Cole suggests that Muhammad was probably literate, as any long-distanced merchant would have been in the seventh century.[19] Long-distance Near East merchants like Muhammad in the latter part of the sixth century would have likely operated in a trilingual environment of Arabic, Aramaic, and Greek.

Muhammad's encounters with Christians during the trading caravans suggest that he may also have had "a very considerable store of knowledge of Judaism and Christianity, and that it was the sort which he would have been most likely to obtain through oral channels and personal observation over a long period of time."[20] In cities like Petra, Muhammad would have learned about Neoplatonic and Christian-Greek styled Arabic notions of love, salvation, and wisdom, which may have piqued his curiosity about Christianity and monotheism at large.[21] Petra had previously been beset by heresies and religious disputes associated with Christianity in the fourth and early fifth centuries. In the sixth and seventh centuries, it served as the capital of Palaestina Tertia (Third Palestine), a Byzantine province and the seat of the metropolitan see of Byzantium.

Muhammad's experiences as a merchant shaped him into a cross-cultural navigator, a sociological term that captures how social identities have been—and continue to be—transformed through cross-cultural exchanges and interactions.[22] A cross-cultural navigator is someone who is able to harvest the resources from their own communities and from wider sociocultural environments. A cross-cultural navigator also conjures up metaphors of traveling and of fluid identities that are constantly in transition. As such, a cross-cultural navigator is someone who possesses insight into—and an understanding of—the functions and values of various cultures across places and times.

Another of Muhammad's cross-cultural encounters occurred around 595, when he is said to have encountered a Christian man named Nestor, who had also been living in Busra. In 595, Muhammad was responsible for leading the trading caravan of a businesswoman named Khadijah bint Khuwaylid (d. 619).[23] Muhammad's relationship with Khadijah ended up transcending business and evolving into a relationship of love. She saw Muhammad not merely as an important business partner or financial asset but a potential husband and life companion. The following description of Khadijah would be acceptable to scholars:

Khadijah was born to a life of privilege. Her family was important in Mecca and quite wealthy; she could have lived a life of ease all her days. Khadijah, however, was an intelligent and industrious young woman who enjoyed business and became very skilled. When her father died, the young woman took charge of her family business, which thrived and grew under her direction. Compassionate as well as hardworking, Khadijah gave a great deal of money to help others—assisting the poor, sick, disabled, widows, orphans, and giving poor couples money to marry. Twice Khadijah married, and when each of her husbands died, she overcame her grief and continued to rear her small children and run her successful caravan business by herself. Khadijah had many employees, including the important position of her agent, who traveled with her caravans, negotiated deals in other cities, and took charge of the large amounts of money involved in the trading business. When Khadijah was 40 years old, she was widely known in Arabia as a powerful, smart, independent woman, and many men wanted to work for her. However, when she needed to hire an agent, she did not hire any of the men who eagerly sought the job. Instead, she selected a hard-working young man named Muhammad who had the reputation of being honest and diligent. Muhammad was only 25 years old when he accepted the job, but he proved to be an excellent employee and a courteous and ethical man.

Khadijah trusted Muhammad so much that she is said to have entrusted him with twice as many goods on trading expeditions as any of his predecessors.[24] She is reported to have possessed half of Mecca's long-distance merchant capital. By all accounts, Khadijah was a disciplined, honorable, and resolute woman.[25]

Returning back to Nestor, Muhammad's encounter with him may have occurred near the same cell as his encounter with Bahira, near the eastern leg of the trading caravan route around fifteen years earlier.[26] Christian cells along the Quraysh's caravan routes may have served as inns for merchants, and Muhammad may have stayed in one.[27]

Like the encounter with Bahira, Muhammad's interaction with Nestor is said to have started while he was resting underneath a tree. Nestor reportedly approached Maysara, an employee of Khadijah and Muhammad's co-worker, and said to her: "Who is the man beneath that tree?" Maysara responded by saying that Muhammad is a man of the Quraysh, of the people who have guardianship of al-Ka'bah. Nestor is reported to have said back: "No one but a prophet has ever sat beneath that tree." Trees are referenced in the Bible as important creations of God and frequent symbols encountered by monotheistic prophets.[28]

What kind of Christian was this man who, like Bahira, referred to Muhammad as a prophet? Nestor was likely a Nestorian, given that his name matched that of Nestorius (d. 450), the archbishop of Constantinople from 428 to 431. In the first year of his bishopric, Nestorius started preaching that Mary (Jesus's mother) should be called "Christokos" (Birth-Giver of Christ) rather than "Theotokos" (Birth-Giver of God). Nestorius, in other words, believed that Mary had given birth to Jesus, which meant that Jesus had to be at least partially human.[29] Nestorius also argued, amid much controversy in the fifth century, that the human person of Jesus died on the cross, but that the divine side of him did not die.

Nestorians, or followers of Nestorius, are referred to as belonging to the Nestorian Church, the name also given to the Syriac Church of the East or the Assyrian Church. The Nestorian Church is thought to have been formed by the Jewish-Christian sects of the Jerusalem Church led in the first century by James (d. 62), the brother of Jesus. A strong Nestorian presence developed in eastern Syria centering on the School of Edessa after the Council of Ephesus (431). Nestorianism is believed to have been commonly practiced in Syria around the late sixth century.[30]

Nestorians were expelled from Edessa in 489 by Emperor Zeno (d. 491) of the Byzantine Empire and emigrated east to the borderlands of Persia.

Rom Landau claims that some of the Lakhmids of Mesopotamia became Nestorian Christians.[31] The Lakhmids were believed to be allies of the Ghassanids, another vassal state of the Byzantine Empire located around Petra and neighboring cities. Nestor, therefore, may have been a Nestorian who was born into the Ghassanid or Lakhmid tribes, or he may have been part of another tribe farther to the east in Mesopotamia or Persia.

The caretakers of Al-Ka'bah

As a member of the Hashim clan, Muhammad and his family members (known as the Hashimites) served as the caretakers of al-Ka'bah, which the Qur'an (3:96) describes as "the first House (of Prayer) established for humankind ... at Bakkah [Mecca], a blessed place and a (center or focus of) guidance for all peoples." According to the Islamic tradition, Abraham (d. 1644 BCE), the biblical figure whose name means "father of many nations," was the builder of al-Ka'bah. He built the structure after arriving in Mecca with Hagar, his mistress, and Ishmael, his eldest son.

While the Hashimites may not have had a lot of material wealth, they were nevertheless respected by other Meccans.[32] Not only did the Hashim clan maintain the peace among the pilgrims at al-Ka'bah but they also sold water, food, and appropriate clothing to the pilgrims who came to worship their gods at the shrine.[33] The Hashimites' role as the caretakers of al-Ka'bah shaped Muhammad into a hospitable and tolerant man who looked after pilgrims and strangers in his midst.

The Hashimites and other clans of the Quraysh decided to rebuild al-Ka'bah, which had fallen into disrepair, when Muhammad was around thirty-five years old. As it stood around

605, the sanctuary had no roof, and the main door of the shrine was difficult to access. The Qurayshites decided to gather wood from a Byzantine merchant ship that had driven ashore and wrecked at Jeddah, a town about 42 miles to the west of Mecca.[34] An unidentified Coptic Christian, or Copt, who had been living in Mecca at the time, is said to have used his carpentry skills to build al-Kaʿbah's roof.[35] The Copts trace their community back to Alexandria, Egypt, and the missionary work of Saint Mark (d. 68), who lived during the reign of Emperor Claudius (d. 54) of the Roman Empire.

As al-Kaʿbah was being rebuilt, the Meccan tribes were competing over which clan would have the honor of lifting the sacred black stone into the corner wall of the shrine. Several of the Qurayshite clans were preparing for warfare against each other after a five-day disagreement. One elder Qurayshite leader is said to have nominated Muhammad to serve as the peacemaker of the dispute, as described below:

> They agreed to follow the old [Qurayshite] man's counsel; and the first man to enter [al-Kaʿbah] was Muhammad ... The sight of him produced an immediate and spontaneous recognition that here was the right person for the task, and his arrival was greeted by exclamations and murmurs of satisfaction. "It is Al-[Ameen]," said some. "We accept his judgment," said others, "it is Muhammad." When they explained the matter to him, [Muhammad] said: "Bring me a cloak." And when they brought it, he spread it on the ground, and taking up the Black Stone he laid it on the middle of the garment. "Let each clan take hold of the border of the cloak," he said. "Then lift it up, all of you together." And when they had raised it to the right height he took the stone and placed it in the corner with his own hands; and the building was continued and completed above it.

Al-Kaʿbah's restoration revealed several important artifacts linked to the monotheistic tradition.[36] The Qurayshites are said to have found a piece of Syriac writing that reportedly read:

I am God, the Lord of [Mecca]. I created her the day I created the heavens and the earth, the day I formed the sun and the moon, and I placed round about her seven inviolable angels. She shall stand so long as her two hills stand, blessed for the people with milk and water.

Beneath the station of Abraham, a small rock near the door of al-Kaʿbah that bears the print of his foot, another piece of writing was discovered. The text read: "Mecca is the holy house of God. Her sustenance cometh unto her from three directions. Let not her people be the first to profane her."[37] These words would be echoed by Muhammad later in his life.

Muhammad would have also learned about the bitter conflict between Byzantium and Persia when he was in his early thirties. In 603, Persian soldiers are said to have entered into Byzantine territory, destroyed entire Christian cities, and killed thousands of Christians. The conflict that ensued, which continued into Muhammad's adulthood, laid waste to a significant portion of the Near East and contributed to the collapse of the Empire's 500-year-long influence in the region.

It was in this complicated and hostile geopolitical environment of warring empires that Muhammad initiated the birth of Islam in a small cave on the outskirts of Mecca.

2

ANGELS AND MYSTICS

Muhammad, now around forty years old, was known by his peers as someone who enjoyed contemplating in isolation, particularly for extended periods of time on Mount Hira, which is known as Jabal an-Nur, the Arabic phrase for "Mountain of Light." Mount Hira lies around 2 miles away from al-Ka'bah. Near the top of the mountain lies a cave that is around 4 and a half yards high and a little more than 1 and a half yards wide.

It is inside this cave that Muhammad experienced the "Night of Destiny," or Laylat al-Qadr, in 610.

The Night of Destiny occurred on an evening during Ramadan, the holy month of the Islamic calendar. Muhammad's experience is considered to be an example of the "mystical Muhammad." A mystic is a person who has the ability to engage in supernatural experiences, namely those that involve apparitions, revelations, and visions. In this context, Muhammad was similar to Christian monks like Bahira and Nestor, both of whom rejected the material world for meditation, soul-searching, and tranquility in their cells in Busra.[1]

Laylat al-Qadr revolves around the presence of Angel Gabriel, whose name is Jibril in Arabic. While the Angel Gabriel is not a

Christian per se, he is an important angel of God that is cited three times in the Bible.[2] Al-Bukhari's collection suggests that Gabriel visited Muhammad 24,000 times, to Jesus ten times, to Abraham forty-two times, and to Moses 400 times.[3] According to the Islamic tradition, no other prophet had more encounters with Jibril than Muhammad.

Muhammad's encounter with Gabriel began while Muhammad was either asleep or in a deep meditative state. Suddenly, the Angel Gabriel entered the cave and hovered over him. Muhammad was stunned by Gabriel's presence and strong embrace, which is reported to have squeezed all the breath from Muhammad's body. Karen Armstrong refers to the Angel Gabriel's hold on Muhammad as a "moment of terror":

> Muhammad could only think that he was being attacked by a *jinni*, one of the fiery spirits who haunted the Arabian steppes and frequently lured travelers from the right path. The *jinn* also inspired the bards and soothsayers of Arabia. One poet described his poetic vocation as a violent assault: [Muhammad's] personal *jinni* had appeared to him without any warning ...[4]

It was during this embrace that Gabriel revealed to Muhammad the opening words of the Qur'an: "Read!" The Arabic word for read, *iqra*, is a root of *qur'an*, which means "recitation."

Muhammad protested Gabriel's commandment by stating: "I do not know how to read."

Gabriel responded by again squeezing Muhammad.

After releasing Muhammad, Gabriel again asked him to recite, to which Muhammad responded a second time: "I do not know how to read."

Yet again, for the third time, Gabriel squeezed Muhammad until he could no longer breathe or bear the pain. Muhammad protested by saying to Gabriel: "I am not a reader."

It was after the third squeeze that Gabriel said to Muhammad: "[Read] in the name of your Lord, who has created all that exists, created man from a clot. [Read]! And your Lord is the Most Generous."[5]

Muhammad became distressed at this seemingly out-of-body experience. On his way down from the cave, he heard a voice that said: "O Muhammad! You are the messenger of God, and I am Gabriel."

Muhammad stood aghast at the angel's presence, and which-ever way he turned, Gabriel was all around him. Finally, the angel disappeared, and Muhammad descended the slope of the mountain to make his way back home.[6]

Muhammad sought the advice and comfort of his wife Khadijah upon arriving in Mecca. He hoped that she would be able to explain what had just happened on Mount Hira.

Upon entering the house, Muhammad fell ill.

"Wrap me up in a blanket! Wrap me up in a blanket!" he said to Khadijah.[7]

Muhammad then told his wife that his experience on Mount Hira could mean one of two things—either he was mad and possessed, or that he was indeed a prophet. Khadijah is said to have responded: "Rejoice, O dear husband, and be of good cheer. You will be the Prophet of this people."

Khadijah not only assured her husband that he was sane but she also encouraged him to trust in God's revelations. In doing so, Khadijah is recognized as the first person to accept the revela-tions received by Muhammad.

A Christian confirms Muhammad's prophethood

To help calm his nerves, Khadijah brought Muhammad to her uncle, Waraqa Ibn Nawfal (d. 610), a Christian who they hoped could make sense of Muhammad's encounter with the Angel Gabriel. Muhammad likely knew Ibn Nawfal before his experi-ence on Laylat al-Qadr, as he may have attended the couple's wedding festivities in 595. Ibn Nawfal is believed to have been the son of Nawfal, the second cousin of 'Abd al-Muttalib, Muhammad's father.[8] If this claim is true, then it would have made Muhammad and Ibn Nawfal distant cousins within the Quraysh tribe. Ibn Nawfal may have even been serving as the leader of the small Christian community of Mecca in 610.

According to Ibn Ishaq, as translated by Alfred Guillaume, when the married couple arrived at Ibn Nawfal's home, Khadijah said to her uncle: "Listen to the story of your nephew, my cousin!"

Ibn Nawfal proceeded to ask Muhammad: "My nephew! What have you seen?" Muhammad then explained his encounter with the Angel Gabriel, to which Ibn Nawfal responded:

> Holy! Holy! ... If you have spoken the truth to me ... there has come to [Muhammad] the great divinity who came to Moses aforetime, and lo, he is the prophet of the people ... This is the same angel who keeps the secrets whom God had sent to Moses. I wish I were young and could live up to the time when your people would turn on you.

Ibn Nawfal concluded by saying: "This is the Law that was revealed to Moses." In uttering these words, Ibn Nawfal is considered to be the "second witness" of Muhammad's claims to prophethood.[9]

After linking him to Moses (d. thirteenth century BCE), the Hebrew prophet and lawgiver of the Jews, Ibn Nawfal told Muhammad: "You will be called a liar, and ill-treated, and they will push you out and make war upon you; and if I live to see that day, God knows I will help His cause."[10] Ibn Nawfal is then said to have leaned toward Muhammad and kissed him on the forehead.

Ibn Nawfal's acceptance of Muhammad's experience on Laylat al-Qadr has been interpreted by some polemicists to be a foreshadowing of Muhammad's prophethood. Mustafa Akyol notes that the original Arabic word for "law" is *namus*, which is the equivalent of the Greek word *nomos*, a term frequently used in the New Testament, especially in Paul the Apostle's letters to the Gentiles, as well as in the Epistle of James. Akyol adds that Ibn Nawfal "seemed to imply that Muhammad was given not just one single revelation of a few words, but a whole divine law for a whole people."[11]

Shortly thereafter, Muhammad and Ibn Nawfal encountered each other at al-Ka'bah in Mecca. Ibn Nawfal was an elderly man at this time and was unlikely to live much longer. Nonetheless, he wished that he could help Muhammad spread Islam to the Meccans. Ibn Nawfal is reported to have died a few days after their encounter at al-Ka'bah.

A *hadith* narrated by A'ishah bint Abu Bakr states that God saved Ibn Nawfal from the hellfire because Muhammad once saw him in a dream wearing white clothing.[12] The *hadith* reads: "Do not slander Waraqa Ibn Nawfal, for I [Muhammad] have seen that he will have one or two gardens in paradise."

Not only was Muhammad defending the honor of his Christian cousin but he was also informing his future believers in Islam that Christians were able to enter heaven.

Who was Waraqa Ibn Nawfal?

Who exactly was this man affirming Muhammad's experience in the cave on Mount Hira? Ibn Nawfal is said to have been a Christian who converted to Christianity while traveling to Syria in the age of *jahiliyah*, the Arabic term referring to the pre-Islamic "age of ignorance."[13]

Ibn Nawfal reportedly converted after reading an Aramaic or Arabic copy of the Gospels. A *hadith* collected by Al-Bukhari states that Ibn Nawfal used to copy and read the Gospel in Arabic. However, this is likely an anachronism, as there is little evidence that a pre-Islamic, Christian version of the Gospels in Arabic ever existed.[14] The oldest surviving text of an Arabic Gospel is dated to around 800 CE, which was probably found at the Mar Saba monastery in Jerusalem. That text resides in the Vatican Library, more commonly known as the Vat, in Vatican City.[15]

Could Ibn Nawfal have mentored and taught Muhammad about monotheism? Scholars typically agree that Muhammad's knowledge of Christianity before Laylat al-Qadr was acquired by word of mouth and not through reading and studying Christian texts. As noted, there was likely no Bible written in Arabic in 610.[16] The Qur'an nevertheless states that Muhammad believed in the Bible, and that, by necessity, all Muslims must believe in too. Consider the following Qur'anic verses:

> The Messenger (Muhammad) believes in what has been sent down to him from his Lord, and so do the believers; each one believes in God, and His angels, and His Books, and His Messengers: "We make no distinction between any of His Messengers (in believing in them)." And they say: "We have heard (the call to faith in God) and (unlike some of the people of Moses) obeyed. Our Lord, grant us Your forgiveness, and to You is the homecoming. (Qur'an 2:285)

> O you who believe! Believe in God and His Messenger (Muhammad) and the Book He has been sending down on His Messenger in parts, and the (Divine) Books He sent down before. Whoever disbelieves in God, and His angels, and His Books, and His Messengers, and the Last Day, has indeed gone astray. (Qur'an 4:136)

> And this (the Qur'an) is a (Divine) Book that We send down— blessed and full of blessing, confirming (the Divine authorship of) whatever was revealed before it—so that you may warn (the people of) the Mother of Cities [Mecca] and those around it. Those who believe in the Hereafter do believe in it; and they are ever mindful guardians of their Prayers. (Qur'an 6:92)

What version of the Bible was Muhammad referring to? The Bible written in Coptic, Greek, Latin, Syriac, or all of these versions?[17] Unfortunately, these questions remain largely unanswered. Some scholars say the Bible that most likely had the

greatest impact, if any impact at all, on Muhammad's understanding of Christianity was written in Syriac and handed down
by Syrian Christians. This version of the Bible, known as the
Peshitta, is said to be the most widely attested and most consistently transmitted of the New Testaments written in Syriac. The
Syriac Church still preserves the Peshitta and holds it in reverence.[18] The Peshitta is also said to have been used by the Monophysites and the Nestorians as a holy text.[19]

Ibn Nawfal may also have used the Gospel of the Hebrews, an
apocryphal text, to teach Muhammad about monotheism, if he
indeed taught him about it at all. In a *hadith* narrated by A'ishah,
as collected by Al-Bukhari, Ibn Nawfal "used to write the writing
with Hebrew letters. He would write from the Gospel in Hebrew
as much as Allah wished him to write." If Ibn Nawfal did in fact
teach Muhammad, he would have served a similar function as
John the Baptist to the coming of Jesus's ministry as explained
in John 3:1–16.

What little we know of Ibn Nawfal has a flare of legend and
often appears to be fashioned as an anachronous example of
Muhammad's prophethood. Some scholars claim that his
encounter with Muhammad after Laylat al-Qadr was fabricated
for the polemical purpose of legitimizing Muhammad's claims as
a monotheistic prophet. Regardless of the veracity of this claim,
Sidney H. Griffith claims that there is no reason to doubt the
reports that Ibn Nawfal was a Christian and that he was familiar
with Jewish and Christian scripture.

The Jewish-Christians

Scholars have also referred to Ibn Nawfal as a "Jewish-Christian."
James, the reported brother of Jesus, is said to have served as the
first leader of the Jewish-Christians, a term used by scholars to
describe a population of Jesus's followers who regarded Jesus as

the Messiah but not as the "Son of God," as Paul the Apostle expressed in his missionary work.[20] James is believed to have promoted the monotheistic faith of Jesus, which was not, necessarily, a faith *about* Jesus.[21]

The Jewish-Christians followed the *halakha*, or Jewish law, and believed in traditional Judaic doctrine. These Jews differed from Paul, a Jew by birth, and his followers in three primary ways. For the Jewish-Christians, God was strictly "one" and not "triune."[22] Jesus was the promised Messiah of the Jews, but not divine, and men could be saved only by two things—faith in God and good deeds.[23] The Jewish-Christian creed may have been best captured by the *Shepherd of Hermas*, a second-century text regarded by the early Christians as a book of revelation. The text states: "First of all, ['Christians'] believe that God is One and that He created all things and organized them and out of what did not exist made all things to be, and He contains all things but alone is Himself uncontained."

The Jewish-Christian population is believed to have gradually experienced an existential decline around the second and third centuries. Traditional Jews viewed them as a runaway sect of Judaism, and the Pauline Christians, also known as the Trinitarians, viewed them as Christian heretics. According to James D. Tabor, a scholar of early Christianity:

> There are two completely separate and distinct [versions of Christianity] embedded in the New Testament. One is quite familiar and became the version of the Christian faith known to billions over the past two millennia. Its main proponent was the apostle Paul. The other has been largely forgotten and by the turn of the first century AD had been effectively marginalized and suppressed by the other ... Its champion was none other than James the brother of Jesus.[24]

As the Jewish-Christians scattered into Arabia, Asia Minor, Egypt, the Hijaz, Persia, and Syria, Pauline Christianity was spreading westward among the European Gentiles, who were creating churches, communities, and documents that eventually became the basis for mainstream Christianity.[25]

Ibn Nawfal may have been an Ebionite, a type of Jewish-Christian. The Ebionites branched out from the original Jewish-Christian community of Jerusalem following the destruction of the Temple of Solomon in 70. Members of this sect were given the name Ebionite after the Hebrew word *ebyonim*, meaning "the poor." They were called Ebionites by their contemporaries because of the alleged "impoverished" opinions they had of Jesus, whom they did not consider to be the Son of God.[26] Followers of Ebionism are said to have regarded Jesus as a prophet of God and as the Messiah, but they also are said to have rejected the claim that he was born to a virgin mother. Joseph A. Fitzmyer further notes that the Ebionites believed in the "'Prophet of Truth' who had a role similar to that of the "Teacher of Righteousness."[27]

The Ebionites are thought to have been discussed by Justin the Martyr (d. 165), who wrote in *Dialogue with Trypho* (150) that some Jews admit that Jesus is Christ while holding him to be "man of men." Scraps of information about the Ebionites are also found in the writing of early Christian writers like Eusebius (d. 339), Irenaeus (d. 202), Jerome (d. 420), Tertullian (d. 240), and Hippolytus (d. 235). These early Christian writers used a strong polemical tone and drew their conclusions about the Ebionites from excerpts of the texts used by Epiphanius (d. 403), who devoted a full chapter to them in a work titled *Panarion* (376).[28] It is practically impossible to draw a clear and historically trustworthy picture of the Ebionite theology.[29] With regard to Ibn Nawfal, there is "really no trace of evidence that he was in fact a member of, or even influenced by, a Jewish Christian community."[30]

Ibn Nawfal may also have been a part of the Essenes, a Jewish sect that has been linked to James and the Jerusalem Church.

Jesus is said to have entered his adult ministry from the remote retreats of men like the Essenes, who adopted an ascetic movement that was critical of the traditional Jewish establishment. The Essenes believed in the sacredness of Israel, but they are also said to have excoriated Israel for having ignored Jewish prophets like Jesus.[31] The Essenes are also believed to be the authors of the Dead Sea Scrolls. These documents, written in the first millennium, revealed an isolated community devoted to studying the text of the known Bible, of which many versions were circulating in the first century.[32] The Essenes may have been working to preserve certain interpretations of Jesus as a prophet rather than the "Son of God."

Ibn Nawfal's recognition of Muhammad's prophethood indicates another possible connection to the Jewish-Christian doctrine of the Elkesaites, who (like the Ebionites) believed in forthcoming prophets and prophecies. The Elkesaites, also spelt "Elchasaites," are believed to have adopted some Jewish-Christian practices in terms of following Judaic law, but the Elkesaites are not believed to have acknowledged Jesus as the Messiah, and they are largely said to have excluded themselves from belonging to the "Universal Church."

The *Book of Elchasai*, the primary text of the Elkesaites, is believed to be an Aramaic text that originated somewhere in eastern Jordan around the year 101. The content of the book is discussed by early Christian scholars, including Epiphanius, Hippolytus, and Origen (d. 254). Out of all the branches of the original Jerusalem Church, the Elkesaites have been identified as the Gnostic sect of early Christianity. The Gnostic sect, or Gnosticism, is rooted in the Greek words *gnosis* (knowledge) and *gnostikos* (good at knowing). The Gnostics were people who believed that the salvation of the soul required knowledge of the mysteries of the universe.

Like the Ebionites, the Elkesaites are said to have believed that a "True Prophet" would reappear among men to call them to the truth. Mustafa Akyol refers to Jesus as the "True Prophet" as prophesized by the Elkesaites; he also claims that their notion of prophecy was "unmistakably similar" to the notion of prophecy as outlined in the Qur'an. If Ibn Nawfal was affiliated or belonged to any of these Jewish-Christian sects, the Elkesaite link seems the most plausible.

The *hunafa'*

Other scholars have identified Ibn Nawfal not as a Christian but more simply as a "believer," which made him a *hanif*, the Arabic term that refers to a person who shunned idol worship and polytheism for monotheism. Muhammad is identified as a *hanif* in his younger and adult life.[33] The plural of *hanif*, the *hunafa'*, is roughly translated to "true believers."

At the time of Laylat al-Qadr, the *hunafa'* are said to have been a small group and loose network of monotheists living around the Arabian Peninsula. The *hunafa'* refused to compromise their beliefs and their frequent outspokenness against polytheism likely relegated them to the fringe of Meccan society. In Mecca, they were respected, tolerated, or ill-treated, depending partly on their individual character and conduct, and also their tribal affiliations.[34]

Ibn Ishaq refers to four *hanif* living in Mecca at the time of Muhammad's birth—Zayd Ibn 'Amir (d. 605), 'Uthman Ibn al-Huwayrith (d. 620s or 630s), Ubayd-Allah Ibn Jahsh (d. 627), and Waraqa Ibn Nawfal (d. 610). Muhammad likely had encounters with all these men.

Ibn 'Amir may have belonged to the Adi clan of the Quraysh tribe. He is said to have denounced polytheism after traveling to Syria to seek out Jewish and Christian scholars, or perhaps even Jewish-Christian scholars. Ibn Habib (d. 859) relates that Ibn 'Amir encountered a Christian monk living in an isolated cell near Balqa, the governorate of Jordan located around 20 miles from Amman. The monk, whose name is not given by Ibn Habib, reportedly told him that he was a *hanif*. The Christian also told Ibn ʿAmir to return to Mecca to witness the rise of Muhammad and Islam.

Ibn Ishaq records that Asma bint Abu Bakr, one of Muhammad's companions, once heard Ibn ʿAmir declare outside al-Kaʿbah: "O Quraysh, none of you is following Abraham's religion except me." Ibn Ishaq also reports that Ibn ʿAmir wrote a poem that reads:

> Am I to worship one lord or a thousand?
> If there are as many as you claim,
> I renounce Al-Lat and Al-ʿUzza, both of them,
> as any strong-minded person would.
> I will not worship Al-ʿUzza and her two daughters ...
> I will not worship Hubal, though he was our lord [in Mecca]
> in the days when I had little sense.[35]

After Ibn ʿAmir's passing in 605, Ibn Nawfal reportedly composed the following eulogy for him:

> You were altogether on the right path, Ibn ʿAmir;
> You have escaped Hell's burning oven
> By serving the one and only God
> And abandoning vain idols ...
> For the mercy of God reaches men
> Though they be seventy valleys deep below the earth.

Another *hanif*, ʿUthman Ibn al-Huwayrith, was part of the Quraysh tribe. He is thought to have converted to Christianity during his visit to Constantinople in 590 to meet with high-ranking Byzantine officials. The reported purpose of his mission was to seek Byzantium's help in setting him up as the sole ruler of Mecca. Following his trip to Constantinople, Al-Huwayrith is said to have returned to Mecca in the hope of convincing the Meccans to allow the Byzantines to annex the city, an annexation that would have made the Meccans subservient to Maurice (d. 602), the Byzantine emperor. The annexation never happened.

Ibn Jahsh, Muhammad's cousin, became interested in mono-theism in the age of *jahiliyah*. According to Ibn Ishaq, Ibn Jahsh embraced Islam and escaped from Mecca during the first *hijra* to the Christian kingdom of Abyssinia, a topic I explore in the next chapter. At Axum, Ibn Jahsh, as reported by Ibn Ishaq, is said to have converted back to Christianity.

Zaid Ibn Harithah, a slave from the Udhra clan of the Kalb tribe of central Arabia, was said to be a *hanif* and the third person to believe in Muhammad's prophethood following Laylat al-Qadr. The Kalb tribe had largely become Monophysite Christians by the sixth century.[36] They also were likely to have been part of the Ghassanids, a satellite nation of the Byzantine Empire in the Levant.[37] Muhammad adopted and freed Zaid after marrying Khadijah, his first wife. Zaid was referred to by Muhammad as al-Habib, the Arabic term for "the Beloved." He was later killed by the Byzantine army at the Battle of Mu'tah (629), which I explore in Chapter 4.

The Qur'an and Islam

In light of Laylat Al-Qadr, the Angel Gabriel's words officially began the process of God's revelations to Muhammad, which is documented in its entirety in the Qur'an. According to the Islamic tradition, as Mona Siddiqui points out, "revelation is to be understood as a process of God communicating in the con-creteness of events, re-igniting in people a new awareness of themselves and their relation to the world."[38]

The Qur'an was not revealed to Muhammad in its complete form on Laylat al-Qadr. It was instead revealed to him from time to time, according to the circumstances, over a period of around twenty-two years. If this timeframe is divided into years of "war" and years of "peace," the period of peace amounts to twenty years. That of war amounts to only two years.

Because Muslims consider the Qur'an to be the literal Word of God, God is thus the author of the Qur'an. Muslims generally believe that the Qur'an is pristine because it was created by God. Muhammad, to be clear, is not the author of the text. He is understood to have served as the messenger of God to bring God's word into the world, through the Qur'an. The Islamic holy text is divided into 114 chapters, or *surahs* in Arabic. Muhammad told his followers that the Qur'an is the only miracle that can be attributed to him. He thus differentiated himself in this regard from Jesus, whom the Qur'an refers to as a miracle worker on many occasions.

In terms of the People of the Book, the Qur'an (3:110) portrays a relatively inclusive notion in relation to their position in the *Ummah*:

> (O Community of Muhammad!) You are the best community ever brought forth for (the good of) humankind, enjoining and promoting what is right and good and forbidding and trying to prevent evil, and (this you do because) you believe in God. If only the People of the Book believed (as you do), this would be sheer good for them. Among them there are believers, but most of them are transgressors.[39]

This Qur'anic verse makes no specific mention of the words "Muslim" or "Islamic" in defining the "community of Muhammad." Shortly after Qur'an 3:110, the Islamic holy text (3:113–15) praises Christians:

> Among the People of the Book there is an upright community, reciting God's Revelations in the watches of the night and prostrating (themselves in worship).

> They believe in God and the Last Day, and enjoin and promote what is right and good and forbid and try to prevent evil, and hasten to do good deeds as if competing with one another. Those are the righteous ones.

Whatever good they do, they will never be denied the reward of it; and God has full knowledge of the God-revering pious.[40]

Perhaps these Qur'anic passages are referring to Bahira, Nestor, Ibn Nawfal, and the other *hunafa* who Muhammad had previously interacted with before Laylat Al-Qadr. Muslims typically believe that the Qur'an is a text that continues the monotheistic traditions of Judaism and Christianity and affirms certain "truths" in the Old and New Testaments, which are gathered together in the Bible.

It is nevertheless important to note that some Muslims believe that there are imperfections and perhaps even errors in the Bible. One argument in defense of this position is that the books of the New Testament were corrupted over time as they were transmitted and compiled into a single book, hence why some Muslims point to the so-called validity of the Qur'an (2:2): "This is the (most honored, matchless) Book: there is no doubt about it (its Divine authorship and that it is a collection of pure truths throughout); a perfect guidance for the God-revering, pious, who keep their duty to God."

But how could Muhammad, who historical sources claimed could not read or write, be the messenger of a grammatically sound and poetic text like the Qur'an? While the traditional Islamic sources portray him as illiterate, other scholars have claimed that he was indeed literate. Juan Cole states that Islamic scholars have traditionally referred to Muhammad as illiterate in order to

protect him from charges by polemicists that he learned things by reading the Bible or other works. But the tradition also says he was a successful long-distance merchant who regularly traded up to Damascus and Gaza in the Eastern Roman Empire. Long distance merchants are always literate, and I think Muhammad could read and write Arabic, Aramaic, and possibly Greek. The Qur'an shows knowledge of the Bible, of Jewish tradition, and of classical Greek thought. It isn't provincial.[41]

Cole's hypothesis challenges the traditional claim that Muhammad is the prophet who communicated God's revelation to humankind both authentically and completely in the Qur'an. Muslims have relied on this perception when defending Islam against those who have attempted to discredit Muhammad and his reception of divine messages.[42]

Muhammad's experience on Laylat al-Qadr also effectively introduced the term Islam to Meccan society. The term Islam is derived from the Arabic word *silm*, which means "to be in peace." The Qur'an states that *as-salam*, which means "peace," is one of the ninety-nine attributes of Allah, the Arabic term for God, who is a manifestation of peace in the Islamic tradition:[43]

> The term [Allah] was a contraction of the article *al*, corresponding to the English word *the*, and the word *ilah*, corresponding to the English word god. Therefore, Allah was not just any god, but "*the* God." Pagan Arabs saw Him as the higher and unseen deity, far above all the other lesser gods that were represented by idols. In this view, Allah was the creator of the heavens and the earth, but he was distant from human beings, which was why humans had to worship the idols.[44]

The idols the Arabs historically worshipped, as the Qur'an (12:40) declares in one of its early verses, were said to be

> but names that you and your forefathers made up for them. (In the absolute sense) judgment and authority rest with none but God alone. He has commanded that you worship none but Him alone. This is the upright, ever-true Religion, but most people do not know (and they act from their ignorance).

The Qur'an (41:30) informs readers that the revelations Muhammad received on Mount Hira were the same kinds of messages that God presented to Abraham, Moses, and Jesus:

> As for those who say, "Our Lord is God," and then follow the Straight Path (in their belief, thought, and actions) without deviation, the angels descend upon them from time to time (in the world

as protecting comrades, and in the Hereafter with the message): "Do not fear or grieve, but rejoice in the glad tidings of Paradise which you have been promised."

The outcast

Like Jesus, Muhammad had stirred up controversy among the natives with his messages and teachings.[45] The Meccans began branding Muhammad as a dangerous outcast after he started publicly sharing God's revelations in 613. He had previously been preaching Islam only in private to his close friends and family members. In the public sphere, Muhammad proclaimed that the various gods worshipped at al-Ka'bah were essentially "false gods." In going public with his teachings, Muhammad became similar to Jesus, as described in the New Testament:

> When [Jesus's] public life becomes controversial, "not even his brothers gave him credence" (John 7:5). Indeed, "[Jesus's] family tried to take him into custody" (Mark 3:21). After making a stir elsewhere, he tried to return to Nazareth, his native village, but the inhabitants "ganged up to throw him out of town, taking him to the edge of the cliff on which the town was built, with the intention of throwing him over" (Luke 4:29).[46]

Some of the Qurayshites were furious that one of their own tribesmen was openly rebelling against their customs and traditions. Some Meccans likely viewed Muhammad as another preacher who was trying to create a moneymaking cult based on a new god that could be worshipped at al-Ka'bah. The Qurayshites may have even believed that he was a "Byzantine spy" or a "secret Jew." Such beliefs may have further rattled the Quraysh, who were then likely dependants of Khosrow II (d. 628), the Persian ruler, with whom some of the Qurayshites were aligned.

Why were the Quraysh so opposed to Muhammad's messages? The Quraysh's settlement in the urban environment of Mecca had made them rich over several generations, and Muhammad was critical of the hyper-material lifestyles that his fellow tribe members had developed over the generations. Mecca's emergence as a trading center triggered a societal shift to materialism that led to an increase in social inequalities, which Muhammad opposed. Huston Smith describes the backlash that Muhammad experienced after introducing Islam to Meccan society:

> [Muhammad's] uncompromising monotheism threatened polytheistic beliefs and the considerable revenue that was coming to Mecca from pilgrimages to its 360 shrines (one for every day of the lunar year); [Islam's] moral teachings demanded an end to the licentiousness that citizens clung to; and its social content challenged an unjust order. In a society riven with class distinctions, the new Prophet was preaching a message that was intensely democratic. He was insisting that in the sight of his Lord all people were equal.[47]

The birth of Islam was a potential sign of monotheism's triumph over polytheism. Muhammad, as Garry Wills points out, was upholding "a new and an embattled cause, just as ancient Jews upheld the worship of the One God, Yahweh, against many idols and their devotees."[48]

Ultimately, Muhammad's encounter with the Angel Gabriel on Laylat al-Qadr ushered in a new worldview for the Meccans. The idea of what it meant to belong to a community of people (what would be known as the *Ummah*, or "nation") was marked by a new moral tone that grew into "a state of mind, a form of consciousness, or an imagined community which united the faithful in order to lead a virtuous life."[49]

The Believers

The messages and words that God revealed to Muhammad were accepted by the "Believers," or al-Mu'minun in Arabic, as the same kinds of words that God had presented to Adam, Noah, Abraham, Moses, David, and Jesus.[50] The Meccans who had accepted Muhammad's teachings were also considered by Muhammad to be Muslim. The term Muslim, which means "one who submits [to God]," is translated from the Arabic word *muslimun*, or "those who submit [to God]." The Qur'an refers to the term *muslimun* (Muslim) in seventy-five instances, yet it refers to Muhammad's followers as al-Mu'minum over 1,000 times. The Islamic holy book also frequently appeals to the Believers (not the Muslims) in the phrase, "O you who Believe."[51]

Mecca in 613 was not particularly safe for Muhammad, the Believers, or the *hunafa'*. These populations were tiny groups worshipping "underground." How, if at all, could Islam's revolutionary message flourish and spread in the unfriendly Meccan climate?

And who, if anyone, could the Believers depend on as allies and friends?

3

ALLIES AND PROPHETS

The hostility that the Believers faced in Mecca reached a tipping point in 614. Hostile acts such as name-calling and petty insults had proven to be ineffective in deterring Muhammad and his followers from practicing Islam. As a result, the Qurayshites decided to develop more sinister tactics, including bullying, harassing, and physically abusing the Believers. Dirt, filth, and stones were tossed at them. Some of the Believers were thrown into prison. Starvation was even used to force them into submission. Other Believers became martyrs for the cause of Islam.

Muhammad himself was the subject of harassment. On one occasion at al-Ka'bah, a man took a handful of dirt and threw it in Muhammad's face and over his head. When Muhammad returned to his home, one of his daughters washed him clean of it, weeping while doing so. He told her: "Do not weep, my little daughter. God will protect your father."[1]

Among the Believers, Bilal ibn Rabah (d. 640) is said to have suffered from some of the harsher forms of persecution. Bilal was the son of Rabah (his father), a slave of Arab descent, and Hamamah (his mother), a former Abyssinian princess. The couple was enslaved to Umayya Ibn Khalaf, the chief of the Jumah clan of Mecca. As the son of Rabah and Hamamah, Bilal was born into slavery. He experienced physical abuse at the hands of Ibn Khalaf after converting to Islam. On many occasions, Ibn Khalaf took Bilal into an open space and tortured him by pinning him to the ground with a large rock on his chest.

Ibn Khalaf tried to force Bilal to renounce Islam and worship Al-Lat and Al-'Uzza, the two gods that Muhammad condemned in front of Bahira the monk, but he remained steadfast in his faith despite being tortured.[2] Bilal would consistently say *Ahad, Ahad,* a reference to "Allah is One" when facing the violence at the hands of Ibn Khalaf.

Muhammad and Bilal were close friends, and the prophet of Islam also considered him to be one of the loyalist Believers. With the assistance of Abu Bakr Abdullah Ibn Uthman (d. 634), another of Muhammad's close companions, Muhammad purchased Bilal's freedom from Ibn Khalaf. Bilal eventually emerged as one of Muhammad's most trusted companions.

Bilal's ancestors, including his mother Hamamah, were royalty in the Christian kingdom of Abyssinia, which extended as far north as northern Ethiopia and as far south as eastern Eritrea around the Horn Africa.[3] Axum, Abyssinia's capital, is believed to be the home of the queen of Sheba, as well as the Ark of the Covenant, which is said to be held in the Church of Our Lady Mary of Zion.[4]

Centuries before Muhammad's birth, the Abyssinians had built an elaborate road network that played an important role in the Christian kingdom's ability to build an empire based on commerce and trading. Axum had access to frankincense, gold, ivory, and leather from throughout the African continent. Mani (d. 277), the prophet and founder of Manichaeism, described Axum as one of the four most powerful kingdoms in the world. By the turn of the sixth century, Axum served as a Byzantine satellite nation and a center of international business.

ALLIES AND PROPHETS

The first hijra

By 615, Muhammad felt that the Believers needed physical safety as living in Mecca was too dangerous.[5] The thirty-ninth chapter of the Qur'an, titled *Surah al-Zumar*, is said to have been revealed to Muhammad in this environment. Ibn Ishaq reports that Muhammad saw the affliction of the Believers and said to them: "If you were to go to Abyssinia (it would be better for you), for the [Christian] king will not tolerate injustice and it is a friendly country, until such time as Allah shall relieve you from your distress." According to Ibn Ishaq, the Believers migrated to Abyssinia with their religion. This was the first *hijra* in Islam, the Arabic term that translates to "migration," which marks the beginning of the Islamic calendar.

Escaping Mecca alive, however, was far from guaranteed. A group of the Believers slipped away from their homes under the dark cover of night, a decision that offered them the chance of escaping alive. Trailing the Believers on horseback were some of the Qurayshite leaders. Thankfully, for the Believers, the desert winds are said to have swirled over their footprints and covered them, thus making it almost impossible to track their movement. Eventually, the Quraysh lost the footprints and were forced to return to Mecca, but only for a brief period of time.

After a long journey across the Arabian Desert, the Believers arrived at Al-Shuaiba, a port close to Mecca, and each Believer is said to have paid a half-dinar to board a ship to cross the Red Sea. The passengers reportedly comprised around eleven men and four women. Among them were Ruqayya bint Muhammad (d. 624), Muhammad's daughter, and Uthman ibn ʿAffan (d. 656), his son-in-law and the third *khalifah* (ruler) of the *Ummah*. Jaʿfar ibn Abu Talib (d. 629), Muhammad's cousin, was also part of the first *hijra*. The first group of Believers to migrate to the Christian kingdom of Abyssinia was later joined by around eighty-three adults.

One can imagine what it might have felt like to be a Believer standing on the dock of Al-Shuaiba. These Believers were a small group of persecuted monotheists who had fled their home in search of freedom of religion. Like Abraham, who told God he would sacrifice anything (even his son) to worship God, the Believers were willing to risk it all.[6] Abraham responded to God's calling by becoming a stranger and starting a voyage. The Believers, too, gave up control over their lives by becoming strangers, and they—like Abraham—never gave up their faith in God.

King Ibn Abjar's allyship

Upon arriving in Abyssinia, the Believers were apprehended by the Abyssinian authorities. They were taken quickly to King Ashama Ibn Abjar (d. 631), the Christian ruler of the Abyssinian Empire. King Ibn Abjar is referred to in Islamic sources as *Najashi*, the Arabic term for "King," but he is also referred to in other sources as King Armah, Ella Tsaham, or simply *Negus*, the Ethiopian term that refers to a monarch or "ruler's reign."[7]

When the Believers arrived at Ibn Abjar's court for questioning, Ja'far, Muhammad's cousin and the leader of the Believers in Abyssinia, presented the king with a letter from Muhammad, which read (in part): "I have sent my cousin Ja'far to you, accompanied by a small number of Muslims; if he comes to you, receive them in hospitality." The Abyssinian king is said to have welcomed the Believers into his kingdom.

Meanwhile, the Qurayshites had learned that Ibn Abjar had allowed the Believers to enter his kingdom. Upon learning this news, the leaders of the Quraysh traveled to Abyssinia to pursue their enemies and demand that the Christian king release Muhammad's followers to them. The Believers would have faced more persecution—and perhaps even death—if they were forced to return to Mecca with the Quraysh.

Two emissaries of the Quraysh—said to be 'Amr Ibn al-'As and Abdullah bin Rabiah—presented gifts to Ibn Abjar in an effort to persuade him and the Abyssinian generals to hand over the Believers. The Qurayshites referred to the Believers as criminal rebels that were trying to overthrow the traditions of Meccan society.

The Islamic tradition refers to Ibn Abjar as a wise leader who was keen on upholding justice and seeking knowledge. He once again summoned Ja'far and the Believers to his court in order to explain the teachings of Muhammad. The Quraysh were granted an audience at the same time. In the presence of his bishops and scholars, Ibn Abjar is said to have asked Ja'far to explain Islam to the Abyssinian Christians. Ja'far said the following in front of them:

> O king! we were plunged in the depth of ignorance and barbarism [before Muhammad's revelations]; we adored idols, we lived in unchastity, we ate the dead bodies, and we spoke abominations, we disregarded every feeling of humanity, and the duties of hospitality and neighborhood were neglected; we knew no law but that of the strong, when Allah raised among us a man, of whose birth, truthfulness, honesty, and purity we were aware; and he called to the Oneness of Allah, and taught us not to associate anything with Him. He forbade us the worship of idols; and he enjoined us to speak the truth, to be faithful to our trusts, to be merciful and to regard the rights of the neighbors and kith and kin; he forbade us to speak evil of women, or to eat the substance of orphans; he ordered us to fly from the vices, and to abstain from evil; to offer prayers, to render alms, and to observe fast. We have believed in him, we have accepted his teachings and his injunctions to worship Allah, and not to associate anything with Him, and we have allowed what He has allowed, and prohibited what He has prohibited. For this reason, our people have risen against us, have persecuted us in order to make us forsake the worship of Allah and return to the worship of idols and other abominations. They have tortured and injured us, until finding no

safety among them, we have come to your country, and hope you will protect us from oppression.

Ibn Abjar responded by asking the Believers if they had brought any scripture with them to Abyssinia. Ja'far then presented to him *Surah Maryam*, the Arabic phrase that translates to "Chapter of Mary." This Qur'anic chapter expresses reverence for Mary, Jesus's mother. Mary is the only woman mentioned by name in the Islamic holy text. The Qur'an may even revere her more than the Gospels.

Unlike the Christian canon, the Qur'an refers to Jesus as the "Son of Mary" instead of the "Son of God." Muhammad also referred to Mary as one of the four most perfect women in world history. Muslims typically believe in her sinlessness and perpetual virginity. The Qur'an (19:16–22) explains her encounter with the Angel Gabriel:

> And make mention, in the Book, of Mary. She withdrew from her family to a chamber (in the Temple) facing east (to devote herself to worship and reflection).
>
> Thus, she kept herself in seclusion from people. Then We sent to her Our spirit, and [Angel Gabriel] appeared before her in the form of a perfect man.
>
> She said: "I seek refuge in the All-Merciful from you, if you are a pious, God-revering one."
>
> He replied: "I am only a messenger of your Lord to be a means (for God's gift) to you of a pure son."
>
> She said: "How shall I have a son, seeing no mortal has ever touched me, and I have never been unchaste?"
>
> He said (quoting God): "Just so. Your Lord says: 'It is easy for Me; and (you shall have a son) so that We make him for humankind a sign (of Our Power on account of his birth) and a mercy from Us (on account of his being a Messenger). It is a matter already decreed.'"

According to Ibn Ishaq, Ibn Abjar "wept until his beard was wet and the bishops wept until their scrolls were wet" after hearing Ja'far read from *Surah Maryam* and other parts of the Qur'an. Ibn Abjar also reportedly said: "These words and the words of Jesus are as rays of light radiating from the same source."

The Qur'an (5:83–5) describes Ibn Abjar weeping after he heard the Believers' praise of Jesus with the following verses:

> When they hear what has been sent down to the Messenger, you see their eyes brimming over with tears because of what they know of the truth (from their own Books); and they say: "Our Lord! We do believe (in Muhammad and the Qur'an); so inscribe us among the witnesses (of the truth in the company of his community). Why should we not believe in God and what has come to us of the truth? And we fervently desire that our Lord admits us among the righteous people." So God (judged that He would) reward them for their saying so with Gardens through which rivers flow, therein to abide. Such is the reward of those who are devoted to doing good, aware that God is seeing them.

The next day, 'Amir Ibn al-'As, one of the Qurayshite emissaries, returned to Ibn Abjar's court to tell him that the Believers held slanderous views about Jesus. Ibn Abjar re-invited the Believers back to his court and is said to have asked them the following question: "What is it that you say concerning Jesus?"

Ja'far stepped forward and stated: "Concerning Jesus we can only say what our Prophet [Muhammad] has taught us: Jesus is the servant and messenger of God, the spirit and word of God, whom God entrusted to the Virgin Mary."[8]

Ibn Abjar was reportedly so inspired by Ja'far's words that he picked up a small stick, drew a line in the sand, then turned to the Believers and said: "I swear, the difference between what we believe about Jesus, the Son of Mary, and what you have said is not greater than this line in the sand."

Ibn Abjar then turned to the Qurayshites and said: "Not for a mountain of gold will I send these people back to Mecca."

He then turned to the Believers and told them: "Go, for you are safe in my country."

In using these words, Ibn Abjar condemned the actions of the Qurayshites and effectively ensured that the Believers were safe to practice Islam in Abyssinia.

While holding firmly to his Christian beliefs, Ibn Abjar did not refute the Qur'anic passages or theological claims read by Ja'far. The Believers had no power over him and posed no threat to the Christians of Abyssinia. Perhaps Ibn Abjar responded to the Believers as a Christian who recognized the legitimacy of Islam, a monotheistic faith that reveres Jesus and Mary.

Instead of condemning Islam at this critical juncture and potentially fateful moment of the first *hijra*, Ibn Abjar accepted and confirmed its existence. A Christian ruler claimed that the Islamic faith was respected and safe in Abyssinia, and that the distinction between Christians and Muslims should be made in only the smallest of terms. Perhaps out of his own awe of God's commandments, Ibn Abjar drew a slight boundary (indeed, a line in the sand) to mark the differences that he saw between Christianity and Islam. That seems quite an important point to consider for Christians and Muslims.[9]

Ibn Abjar also did not busy himself with charges of heresy or with attempts to convert the Muslims to Christianity but instead focused on being an ally and engaging in allyship, or the process of acting in solidarity with those who have experienced discrimination, marginalization, and violence. The Believers, on the other hand, could have dismissed the Abyssinian Christians as adversaries and apostates and presented them with the choice to convert or be eliminated, but they did not.[10] Ibn Abjar and the Abyssinian theologians in his court appeared to believe that both expressions of faith originated from the same source—God. The Arabic Allah of the Believers appeared to be the same as the God of the Abyssinians.

The Christians of Abyssinia

Who exactly were the Christians of Abyssinia? Samuel Zinner traces Abyssinia's Christians back to the Ebionites, who, together with their Jewish compatriots, fled the Roman Empire's destruction of Jerusalem in 70 CE.[11] Zinner describes the Abyssinian Christians as having unmistakable Jewish practices including the observance of the Sabbath and the circumcision of males. However, the Church of Abyssinia, and subsequently the Christian kingdom that had jurisdiction over it, reportedly accepted the rulings of the Council of Nicaea.[12] The Council of Nicaea's ruling was that Jesus is divine, consubstantial, of one-being or essence with God (the Father), and human (he was incarnate and became man on earth). This declaration became the first-ever uniformed and universal Christian doctrine—the Trinity, which was made up of the Father (God), the Son (Jesus), and the Holy Spirit.[13] The following proclamation from the final ruling is referred to as the Nicene Creed or the Apostles' Creed:

> [Christians] believe ... in one Lord Jesus Christ, the only Son of God, begotten from the Father before all ages. God from God, Light from Light, true God from true God, begotten, not made; of the same essence as the Father. Through him all things were made. For us and for our salvation he came down from heaven; he became incarnate by the Holy Spirit and the Virgin Mary, and was made human. He was crucified for us under Pontius Pilate; he suffered and was buried. The third day he rose again, according to the Scriptures. He ascended to heaven and is seated at the right hand of the Father. He will come again with glory to judge the living and the dead. His kingdom will never end.

There is little doubt that the closing statement of the Nicene Creed had Arius in mind, as it reads:

> But as for those who say, there was when He was not, and, before being born He was not, and that He came into existence out of

nothing, or who assert that the Son of God is from a different ... substance, or is created, or is subject to alteration or change—these the Catholic [that is, Universal] Church anathematizes.[14]

The Qur'an refers to these Christological developments as the "sin of sins."[15] While the Qur'an clearly reveres Jesus as a prophet and the Messiah, it also rejects his divinity—a belief that Islam's strict monotheism can never accept.[16]

Muslims do not typically believe that Jesus died on the cross, as Christians generally believe. The Qur'an also does not report that Jesus died a natural death, but that he instead ascended to heaven where he will remain until he returns to earth on the Day of Judgment. Muslims, moreover, generally do not believe that Jesus is God because he never claimed to be God. The popular "Islamic narrative" is that Jesus's followers, in the centuries following his passing, began to assign attributes to him that were semi-divine, if not outright divine.

It is also worth pointing out that according to Islamic theology in general, Jesus did not introduce and reveal new religious laws, or reform earlier laws as given to previous prophets. He instead introduced a new *Tariqah*, the Arabic term for "path" or "way," based on the love of God.[17] It is perhaps for this reason that Jesus has been adopted by the mystics, or Sufis, of Islam. The Sufi philosopher Al-Ghazali (d. 1111) described Jesus as "the prophet of the soul" and the Sufi master Ibn 'Arabi (d. 1240) called him "the seal of the saints."[18]

Despite these points of differentiation, there were harmonious relations between the Believers and the Christians of Abyssinia, and differences over Jesus's nature did not prevent the Christians from protecting the Believers from the Qurayshites. The Believers, on the other hand, did not allow Christological disagreements to interfere with their desire to build a bridge with the Christians of Abyssinia.

ALLIES AND PROPHETS

The Night Journey to Jerusalem

Meanwhile, back in Mecca, Muhammad and his fellow Hashimites suffered from a boycott implemented by the Quraysh, their own tribal members. The Qurayshite leaders even put a bounty of 100 camels on Muhammad's life.

The prophet's standing in Mecca had plunged even further by 619, arguably the most difficult year of his life, one referred to as the "Year of Sorrow." Khadijah had passed away. Not only was she Muhammad's wife, but she was the mother of their four daughters. To make matters worse for Muhammad, Abu Talib, his uncle and guardian, passed away in the same year. Abu Talib's passing meant that he could no longer act as a buffer between Muhammad and the Believers and the Qurayshite leaders.

And yet two years after the Year of Sorrow, the city of Jerusalem emerged as a source of inspiration for Muhammad. Muslims typically refer to Jerusalem as Al-Quds, or "the Holy One," the city in which God is said to have issued the first ray of light from the Rock, the site where Abraham attempted to sacrifice his son. The Rock is hidden under the Golden Dome, known as the Dome of the Rock, or *Qubbat al-Sakhrah* in Arabic. For Muslims, Jerusalem served as the original *qiblah*, or the prayer direction, until Muhammad changed the direction toward al-Ka'bah in Mecca around 624.

Jerusalem served as Muhammad's source of inspiration through his "Night Journey to Jerusalem" (621), another mystical experience like the one that occurred on Laylat al-Qadr.[19] The Night Journey to Jerusalem is the combination of two events—the Isra (the Arabic term for "Night Journey") and the Mi'raj (the Arabic term for "Ascension").[20] These events contained many biblical figures that are familiar to Christians.

The Isra begins on a night when Muhammad, who was sleeping near al-Ka'bah, was visited again by the Angel Gabriel,[21] who woke Muhammad and brought him to Zamzam, where Muhammad's heart was taken out of his chest and split open. His heart was then washed and filled with belief and wisdom, before it was returned inside his body. Buraq, a half-mule and half-donkey that is likened to a supernatural animal with wings on the sides of its body, was presented to Muhammad as a mount. On the back of Buraq, they departed Mecca and traveled to Yathrib, where Muhammad offered prayers. The Angel Gabriel told him that he would one day migrate to the city, a migration that I explore in the next chapter. After praying in Yathrib, Gabriel and Muhammad, on the back of Buraq, traveled to Bethlehem, the city in which Jesus was born.

Following the visit to Bethlehem, the Angel Gabriel guided Muhammad to the ruined Temple of Solomon in Jerusalem. At Solomon's temple, Buraq was tied to the ring to which the mounts of previous prophets were tied. Gabriel then introduces Muhammad to Abraham, Moses, Jesus, and other biblical figures. Inside the Temple, Muhammad is reported to have led the prophets in prayer.

The Mi'raj, the second part of the journey, also involves Buraq and Gabriel. In Jerusalem, Muhammad received a ladder, which he then proceeded to climb alongside the angel. Together, they climbed its rungs and eventually reached the gate of heaven, where they are said to have been greeted by Ishmael, the oldest son of Abraham.

Ishmael asked Gabriel at the gate of heaven: "Has this person [Muhammad] received a message?"

Gabriel responded by affirming, "Yes." Ishmael then allowed Muhammad and Gabriel to enter heaven.

Ishmael is an important link between Jews, Christians, and Muslims, the three populations that make up the Abrahamic tradition. Although he is only mentioned twelve times in the Qur'an, the Islamic holy text states that Ishmael "was one always true to his promise, and was a Messenger, a Prophet. He used to enjoin on his people the Prayer and the Prescribed Purifying Alms, and he was one favored and pleasing in his Lord's sight" (Qur'an 9:54–5). The Qur'an adds that the Quraysh are descended from Ishmael, who the book says had settled in Mecca in the third century BCE. Ishmael became the progenitor of the Arabs. Isaac, Abraham's other son, became the patriarch of the Israelites, who are said to have remained monotheists throughout the generations.

The Arabs, on the other hand, had slipped into polytheism by worshipping multiple gods in the form of idols and statues. It was Muhammad's destiny and task to bring the Arabs back to their monotheistic origins. This destiny was confirmed by Ibn Nawfal, who told Muhammad that his life's mission was to bring the Mosaic Law to his people, the Arabs.

Muhammad was greeted by Adam, the Old Testament figure of the Adam and Eve story, with the greeting of "peace be with you," or *as-salamu 'alaykum* in Arabic, in the first stage of heaven. Adam identified Muhammad as a prophet, and Muhammad, in turn, witnessed how Adam served as a judge of the departed souls from Earth.

The Qur'an, like the Bible, refers to Adam as the first human being created by God. Adam was expelled from the Garden of Eden, his first habitat, but is nevertheless considered in the Islamic tradition to be the first prophet and the first bearer of the monotheistic covenant with God. According to the Islamic tradition, he was also the first human being to proclaim that there are no other gods but God. As the first prophet, Adam is considered by some Muslims to be the "first Muslim."

Muhammad also interacted with Malik, an angel serving as the gatekeeper of hell in the first stage of heaven. He showed Muhammad the flames of hell as a warning sign to never sin. After meeting Malik, the prophet of Islam then ascended to the second stage of heaven. The Angel Gabriel gave Muhammad permission to enter the gate. Upon entering, Muhammad interacted with two men who looked like brothers because of their similar physical appearance.

These figures were none other than Jesus and John the Baptist, who were cousins. Muhammad greeted them both by saying *as-salamu 'alaykum*. Jesus and John responded to him by saying: "May peace be with you, too."

According to a *hadith* narrated by Abu Huraira, one of the prophet's companions, Muhammad equated himself with Jesus in the second stage of heaven when he stated: "Both in this world and in the Hereafter, I am nearest of all the people to Jesus, the son of Mary. The prophets are paternal brothers; their mothers are different, but their religion is one."

The Qur'an refers to Jesus as a messenger and prophet of God who had brought a divine message for all human beings. He is identified in the Islamic holy text as the "Word" and "Spirit" of God. No other prophet in the Qur'an, not even Muhammad, is described in this way. On eleven occasions, the Qur'an declares that Jesus is the only *Masih*, the Arabic term for "Messiah." Jesus is arguably the most revered figure in the Qur'an.[22]

John (the Baptist), whose name is Yahya in Arabic, is one of the twenty-five prophets mentioned by God in the Qur'an. Like Jesus, his birth is considered to be a miracle in the Islamic tradition. Elizabeth, his mother, was said to be barren, and Zachariah, his father, was considered to be too old to have a child. The Qur'an (21:89–90) informs readers to consider Zachariah among the prophets of monotheism:

> [Mention also] Zachariah. Once he called out to his Lord, saying: "My Lord! Do not let me leave the world without an heir, for You are the Best of the inheritors."

> We answered his call, too, and bestowed upon him John, and cured his wife for him (so she was able) to bear a child. Truly, these (three)

used to hasten to do good deeds as if competing with each other, and invoke Us in hopeful yearning and fearful anxiety. And they were utterly humble before Us.

Joseph, the Old Testament figure and prophet according to the Qur'an, greeted Muhammad at the gate of the third stage of heaven. Also known as Yusuf in Arabic, Joseph serves as a link between the Bible and the Qur'an, which share a similar version of his story. The Qur'an's version is documented in an entire Qur'anic chapter that is around 100 verses long, making it the longest single story in the Islamic holy text.[23]

Muhammad encounters Enoch, the ancestor of Noah (the biblical figure), in the fourth stage of heaven. Enoch welcomes Muhammad as Joseph did before him. Muslim scholars typically identify Enoch as Idris, the Arabic term meaning "interpreter," because of his commitment to studying the scripture linked to Adam and Seth, his prophetic ancestors. Al-Tabari credits Idris with possessing special abilities in gaining knowledge. Ibn Arabi calls Idris the "prophet of the philosophers," and Ibn Ishaq reports that Idris was the first human being to write with a pen.

Aaron (d. 1273 BCE), Moses's older brother, a prophet, and the first high priest of the Israelites, is the guardian of the fifth stage of heaven. Ibn Hisham wrote about Muhammad's wonderment at seeing Aaron, or Harun in Arabic. Muhammad said that Aaron's face had the splendor of the moon at its full, and that he had been endowed with no less than half of all the existing beauty in the world. The Eastern Orthodox churches venerate Aaron as a saint, and the Armenian Apostolic Church commemorates him as one of the Holy Forefathers in their Calendar of Saints. The Qur'an identifies Aaron as a prophet of God and praises him with phrases and terms like "clear signs," "manifest authority" (Qur'an 23:45) and "We showed him the Straight Path" (Qur'an 37:118). The Islamic holy text also describes both Aaron and Moses as being sent together by God to warn the Pharaoh about God's punishment (Qur'an 10:75). The Qur'an (10:87) adds that the brothers were tasked by God with creating monotheistic places of worship.

Muhammad then proceeds to the sixth stage of heaven to meet Moses (or Musa in Arabic), the Hebrew lawgiver and prophet of Islam. Moses is reported to have cried upon Muhammad's arrival. When Muhammad asked him why he was crying, Moses reportedly said: "I weep because after me there has been sent a young man, whose followers will enter paradise in greater numbers than my followers."

Moses was referring to Muhammad.

As the representative of the chosen people dealing directly with God on Mount Sinai, Moses is the most often mentioned or described person in the Islamic holy text.[24] Moses is described as having been spoken to directly by God. Allah also revealed to him knowledge, as explained in Qur'an 7:145, which provided the Israelites with divine law:

> (Moses completed the term appointed by his Lord for him to be favored with the Book to order his people's affairs). And We recorded for him on the Tablets whatever is necessary as instruction and guidance (to follow the way to God), and as explanation for all matters. And (We said): "Hold fast to them with strength, and command your people to hold fast to the best thereof (fulfill the commandments in the best way possible). I will soon show you the (ultimate) abode of the transgressors."

Muhammad then travels through the gate of the seventh stage of heaven, where Abraham greets and welcomes him while sitting at the throne of paradise. Abraham is the great patriarch of the Hebrew Bible and the spiritual forefather of the New Testament, as well as the architect of the Qur'an.[25] As such, Abraham is the centerpiece and shared ancestor of Judaism, Christianity, and Islam. The Qur'an (3:95) in particular calls on readers to "follow the way of Abraham as people of pure faith (a faith free of unbelief, of associating partners with god, and of hypocrisy). He was never of those who associated partners with God." While Muhammad may be more important for Muslims, Jesus for Christians, and Moses for Jews, all three traditions link themselves back to Abraham, the common mono-theistic patriarch. Abraham unites the Ahl al-Kitab.

Ibn Ishaq also reports that Muhammad said the following in the seventh stage of heaven: "I saw a damsel with dark red lips and I asked her to whom she belonged, for she pleased me much when I saw her, and she told me 'Zaid, son of Haritha.'" Zaid was the adopted son and close companion of Muhammad who may have been a Christian before converting to Islam. Zaid's presence in heaven mirrors the Qur'an (5:85), which suggests that Christians would be rewarded with gardens in heaven through which rivers flow.

Ibn Ishaq concludes the story by writing that Muhammad was ultimately welcomed into paradise by God. Muhammad then returned to Mecca, thus ending the Night Journey.

Muhammad's transcending of time, space, and community, as Karen Armstrong claims, "celebrated harmony, transcendence of the blood group, and integration with the rest of humanity."[26] Armstrong added

> Muhammad was abandoning the pagan pluralism of Mecca, because it had denigrated into the self-destructive arrogance and violence of *jahiliyah*, but he was going to embrace monotheistic pluralism. In Jerusalem he discovered that all the prophets, sent by God to all peoples, are "brothers." Muhammad's prophetic predecessors do not spurn him as a pretender, but welcomed him into their family. The prophets do not revile or try to convert each other; instead they listen to each other's insights. They invite the new prophet to preach to them and, in one version of the story, Muhammad asks Moses for advice about how frequently Muslims should pray ... The fact that this appreciation of other traditions is written into the archetypal

myth of Muslim spirituality shows how central this pluralism was to early Islam.[27]

Similarly to Armstrong, John Baldock describes the Isra and Mi'raj as an "inner, mystical occurrence."[28] Ronald Rolheiser, a scholar on religious mysticism, claims that these experiences may have been lucid and clear dreams rather than "real world" events. Other scholars have argued that Muhammad's spirit—not his physical body—ascended to the seven stages of heaven.

Cole, however, contends that Muhammad may have physically traveled overland to Jerusalem. Which Christian populations could Muhammad have encountered on this hypothetical overland journey? It is plausible that he interacted with Arab Christians in Jerusalem, the Arab Christians of the Banu Judham near Jericho, and the Ghassanids farther south in the Levant. The Judham Christians are reported to have lived in northwestern Arabia, a region that fell into the Byzantine Empire's sphere of influence from the fifth to the eighth centuries. Cities controlled by the Judham included 'Amman, Ma'an, Madyan, Tabuk, Udhruh, and Wadi Al-Qura.

The Fall of Jerusalem and Emperor Heraclius of Byzantium

If Muhammad did in fact physically travel overland to Jerusalem, he may also have listened to reports about Shahrbaraz, a general of the Persian Empire who conquered Jerusalem in 614. Shahrbaraz is said to have massacred thousands of Christians, burned churches, and captured Patriarch Zachariah, the leader of the Jerusalem Church.[29] The Persian general also reportedly confiscated the True Cross, the name given to the physical remnants of the cross upon which Jesus is said to have been crucified. The True Cross was reportedly discovered in 326 by Helena (d. 330), the mother of Emperor Constantine, in Jerusalem.[30]

What else might Muhammad have seen in Jerusalem while it was under Persian rule? Sophronius (d. 638), the patriarch of

Jerusalem and contemporary of Muhammad, said that the Christians lamented their loss in 614 to the Persians on the Jerusalem Hills. The Persian advance made war on Byzantine cities and towns, a conflict that is said to have alarmed Emperor Heraclius (d. 641) of Byzantium. Soon after sacking Jerusalem, the Persians moved on to conquer parts of Egypt and Syria and are even said to have reached as far westward as Constantinople, the capital of Byzantium and the center of Christendom. The Persians, however, did not conquer the city.

Heraclius ruled the Rum, the Arabic term that refers to the Byzantine Empire, from 610 to 641. The Qur'an calls the "Roman land" the Rum and the Romans as Ar-Rum.[31] The Islamic holy text, however, is referring largely to the Byzantine Christians of Constantinople rather than the Roman Christians of Rome.[32] Constantine moved the Roman Empire's capital from Rome to Byzantium, the ancient Greek town that he renamed Constantinople, in 330.[33] Constantinople emerged as the more powerful city due largely to the Visigoths sacking Rome in 410.

According to John F. Haldon, Heraclius is "popularly and probably quite justifiably regarded by both modern historians and by Byzantines as one of the empire's greatest rulers."[34] Islamic sources state that Heraclius served the cardinal function of recognizing and acknowledging the prophetic character and mission of Muhammad and the *Ummah*, a topic I return to in Chapter 6.[35] Heraclius is known for receiving the overwhelming approval of Muslim historians, who bestowed upon him distinguished abilities and attributes.[36] Ibn Kathir, for example, praised him in glowing terms: "Heraclius was one of the wisest men and among the most resolute, shrewd, deep and opinionated kings. He ruled the Byzantines with great leadership and splendor."[37]

By the early 620s, during Heraclius' rule, the Believers were situated between two rival empires—Byzantium and Persia—both of which had zig-zagged their way around the Arabian

Peninsula for centuries. The Byzantines dominated the areas of Asia Minor, but they struggled to prevent the Persians from invading Armenia and Syria, their easternmost territories. The Persians largely controlled the areas around the Tigris and Euphrates River in the Fertile Crescent and parts of the Arabian Peninsula's coasts.

The Byzantines and Persians were bent upon mutual destruction. Juan Cole refers to the Byzantine–Persian entanglement around the Arabian Peninsula as a kind of "game of thrones," a reference to *Game of Thrones*, the HBO drama series documenting a fictional web of alliances and conflicts between dynasties, all of which fought for supreme control of the known world.[38]

How did Muhammad and the Believers handle their precarious situation of being squeezed in-between empires?

And how could Muhammad's movement survive amid these geopolitical developments?

4

CITIZENS AND REBELS

The Night Journey to Jerusalem marked a turning point in Muhammad's life. He now had deeper faith in his mission as a prophet, a role that was similar to the missions of the previous monotheistic prophets as documented in the Bible and the Qur'an. Muhammad's task was to believe in monotheism, praise God, and uplift humanity.

But Muhammad faced significant barriers and challenges in trying to follow these tasks in Mecca. He and the Believers needed a fresh start. Where, if anywhere, could they effectively practice Islam?

Yathrib, which was later renamed Medina by the Believers, emerged as their safe haven, albeit only for a period of time. The town was located around 200 miles to the north of Mecca. Muhammad and the Believers migrated there in 622, the year of the second *hijra* of the early *Ummah*. While the Believers were seeking their new start, Emperor Heraclius of Byzantium started his counterattack into Asia Minor and its surrounding territories to recover territory lost to the Persian Empire in the previous decade.[1]

Arriving in Yathrib safely was no trivial matter for Muhammad. He slipped away in the middle of the night and headed south, in the opposite direction of Yathrib, in order to avoid alerting the Qurayshites of his final destination. At best, the Quraysh would have prevented Muhammad from making the journey to Yathrib. At worst, they would have killed him if they had captured him.

Abu Bakr, Muhammad's closest companion and the second *khalifah* of the *Ummah*, accompanied Muhammad on the journey to Yathrib. The two friends are said to have hid for three days at Jabal Thawr, or Mount Bull, inside a cave known as Ghar Sawr, or Cave of Sawr, which is located around 3 miles from al-Ka'bah.

Soon after Muhammad and Abu Bakr had escaped from Mecca, a group of Quraysh horsemen set out to capture them. The Qurayshites searched far and wide and are said to have come close to discovering them inside the cave. Upon feeling that they were close to being captured, Abu Bakr is reported to have said to Muhammad: "We are only two people." Abu Bakr was concerned that the two men would be unable to defend themselves against the larger Qurayshite force of horsemen.

Muhammad is reported to have said to Abu Bakr: "No, we are three, for God is with us."

On the fourth day of hiding, Muhammad and Abu Bakr left the cave unscathed and finally headed toward Yathrib. The Believers followed thereafter.

Yathrib's conflict

In 622, Yathrib was populated by around 10,000 people who belonged to about twenty-two tribes. Half of the Yathribite population is thought to have been Jewish, and perhaps more specifically Arab Jews whose ancestors had converted to Judaism.[2] Some of the Jewish elders among the Yathribite tribes were serving in leadership positions in Yathrib.[3]

Yathrib's powerful groups included three Jewish tribes—the Nadir, Qaynuqa, and Qurayza. These Jewish groups likely arrived in this part of northern Arabia no later than the fourth century. The other half of the Yathribite population is said to have been Arab polytheists, who were following a range of deities and gods in a similar way to the Meccans.[4] Toward the end of the fifth century, the Aws and Khazraj—two Arab tribes—took control of Yathrib after a revolt.[5]

Members of the Khazraj, some of whom may have been familiar with Christianity, officially joined the Believers upon Muhammad's arrival. Juan Cole claims that the Khazraj may have had previous ties to the Ghassanids, who were Christians and allies of Byzantium at the time. He also suggests that the Khazraj may have been looking to the Believers for allyship in order to further liberate themselves from the Persian Empire to the east.[6]

Relations between the powerful tribes of Yathrib—among them the Aws, Khazraj, Nadir, Qaynuqa, and Qurayza—hit rock bottom in the seventh century. Unsettled tribal feuds had escalated over access to key resources, control of aquifers, and disputes over land cultivation.[7] The Yathribites were also entangled in alliances and immersed in complicated power dynamics. The Aws are said to have been allied with the Nadir and Qurayza, while the Khazraj were allied with the Qaynuqa.[8] Yetkin Yildirim describes the tribal dynamics upon Muhammad's arrival in Yathrib:

> Generations of fighting had been taking their toll on many peace-loving tribal members. While some sought external military assistance, which only exacerbated the conflicts, many were making preparations for the enthronement of 'Abdallah ibn Ubay Ibn Salul. However, it was unlikely that the independent rulers of each tribe would acquiesce to the leadership of a single king. It was also unclear whether a king would be able to establish a political organization,

create a military [defense] for the city, reconcile tribal hostilities, define local rights and obligations, and address the issues of the growing immigrant refugee population from Mecca.[9]

In 622, the main source of conflict in Yathrib centered on a feud between the Aws and Khazraj. The Battle of Bu'ath (617) had been their most recent engagement in warfare. The two leading Arab tribes had asked Muhammad to mediate their conflict in order to bring peace to Yathrib. Mediation was a common practice among the Yathribite Jews, who were likely following the practices of *bizuah* (mediation) and *p'sharah* (arbitration) according to the Talmudic law. The *bizuah* and *p'sharah* were also common practices among the Arab tribes.[10]

If the Qur'an had no law to deal with the conflict between the Aws and Khazraj, Muhammad would use his own reasoning as guided by divine inspiration.[11] This is the principle known as *ijtihad*, the Arabic term referring to "independent reasoning." A second principle Muhammad used to mediate the conflict rested on *istislah*, which is judgment concerned with decisions made in the best interest of the community.

How could an outsider like Muhammad bring peace to the generations-long tribal conflict in Yathrib?[12] For starters, he is said to have created a sanctuary zone in the town so that none of the tribes would enter into armed conflict. This sanctuary zone banned hunting, cutting down trees, and carrying weapons. Muhammad likely borrowed this tactic from his own Hashim clan, the protectors of al-Ka'bah, who were responsible for keeping the peace among the pilgrims traveling to and worshipping at the ancient sanctuary.

Muhammad is likely to have periodically resided in the homes of either the Aws or Khazraj upon his arrival in Yathrib. To help him better blend in with the Yathribite population, the Believers built him an ordinary house shortly after his arrival. Muhammad is not said to have relied heavily on any servants. Instead, he is reported to have carried out his own laborious tasks, including cleaning his own clothes and milking his own goats.

Upon arriving in Yathrib, the Believers were also tasked with creating a place of worship, or *masjid*. The *masjid* that they built was a humble and simple building. In the middle of the building's northern wall, which the Believers named the "Jerusalem Wall," were stones on both sides of the prayer niche. Muhammad and the Believers used to pray three times per day by turning their bodies toward Jerusalem.[13]

The Christians of Yathrib

Christians are likely to have lived in Yathrib at the time of Muhammad's arrival in 622.[14] Muhammad Hamidullah estimates that the Christian population of the city may have been in the thousands.[15] Unfortunately, there is little knowledge available on the Christians of Yathrib before the second *hijra*. Archaeological evidence of Christian monastic life in Kilwa, a town just south of Transjordan and around 375 miles to the north of Yathrib, points to a potential outpost for the ancient Christians of Yathrib.[16]

Abu 'Amir Al-Rahib is the most well-documented Christian during this period of Yathrib's history.[17] Al-Mas'udi and Ibn Sa'd state that he was of the Aws, while Ibn Kathir reports that he had a high place among the Khazraj; it is not clear, as Ghada Osman points out, whether this last statement actually means that Abu 'Amir was of the Khazraj or just that he was respected among them, despite being from the warring Aws.[18] Al-Mas'udi reports that Abu 'Amir followed the Christian religion of Heraclius of Byzantium and that he was sometimes called "the Monk." Al-Baladhuri (d. 892 CE) adds that Abu 'Amir was a Christian monk who had joined Jewish and

Christian trading caravans to Syria.[19] Much later scholars like Lings claim that Abu 'Amir had acquired religious authority among the Yathribites.[20]

Abu 'Amir is reported to have visited Muhammad in Yathrib after his arrival in the town in 622. Sources say that he told Muhammad that he had falsified the Abrahamic faith. Muhammad reportedly replied: "I have not, but I have brought it white and pure." To which Abu 'Amir responded: "May God let the liar die a lonely outcast exile!" "So be it," Muhammad is reported to have replied. "May God do that unto him who is lying!"

Another Yathribite—Salman al-Farisiy (d. 653)—is said to have been a Christian living in Yathrib at the time of the second *hijra*. Reportedly born with the name Roozbeh or Ruzbeh, Salman is believed to have belonged to a Zoroastrian family from the village of Jayy near Isfahan, a province of the Persian Empire. Around 587, Salman is said to have embraced Nestorianism as a young man while traveling to Syria.[21] Lings notes that Salman had studied under a Christian bishop of Syria, who, on his deathbed, told him to visit the bishop of Mosul. In Mosul, Salman reportedly studied under a Christian philosopher, who, also on his deathbed, told him that a prophet of the religion of Abraham would arise out of the Arabian Peninsula and settle in a place between two lava tracts, a country of palms, a description that fits Yathrib's location.

The dying Christian philosopher also told Salman that this prophet will eat of a gift but not if it be given as alms; and between his shoulders is the seal of prophecy, a prediction that mirrors Bahira's signaling of the seal of prophecy near Muhammad's shoulder.

On his journey back to Persia, Salman was captured and enslaved by a Jewish man of the Qurayza tribe. Salman's experience as a slave came in handy at the Battle of the Trench, which I examine in a forthcoming section.

CITIZENS AND REBELS

The Constitution of Medina

Muhammad's role as the mediator of Yathrib's tribal conflicts was different from the role he had previously played in Mecca. He was no longer necessarily serving merely as a prophet but rather as a judge and even a statesman. Muhammad, as Armstrong describes him at this point in his life, "could not simply withdraw from the mainstream. He had to put God's revealed will into practice and create a just, egalitarian society."[22]

As Yathrib's new leader, Muhammad focused on the difficult task of administering and governing the multicultural and multireligious Yathribite population. Muhammad's first meeting with the Yathribites occurred in the home of Anas in Aqaba, a neutral setting and town near Mecca. Ten tribes in total are reported to have been at the initial council. The Aws and Khazraj were the most powerful voices in the meeting. The Qurayza were also heavily involved in the negotiations, which were intended to charter a new legal and political framework for the Yathribites. The Nadir and Qaynuqa are also believed to have been present. If Christians were involved in the initial council, they may have been part of the Jaffna clan of the Tha'aba tribe.[23]

As the meeting's chairman, Muhammad listened to the grievances of the tribes and suggested a course of action to settle the feuds. The parties involved in the council ultimately agreed on a legal and political framework called the Constitution of Medina (see appendix 2).[24] Yildirim summarizes the agreement as follows:

> [The Constitution of Medina] outlined the rights and duties of citizens, provided collective protections for all citizens of [Yathrib] including both Muslims and non-Muslims, and implemented the first means of seeking justice through law and community as opposed to tribal military actions. It also addressed specific social issues of the community in an attempt to regulate the tribal conflicts that had been plaguing the region for generations.[25]

To usher in this new way of life, Muhammad renamed Yathrib Al-Madina al-Munawwarah (The Enlightened City).[26]

The Constitution of Medina had a total of forty-seven articles.[27] Each article addressed a specific conflict among the Yathribite tribes. The first twenty-three articles are concerned with the agreements between the Believers and the Aws and Khazraj, who became known as the al-Ansar, the Arabic term for "the Helpers." The Qur'an (9:100) praises the partnership formed between the Believers and the Helpers:

> The first and foremost (to embrace Islam and excel others in virtue) among the [Believers] and the Helpers, and those who follow them in devotion to doing good, aware that God is seeing them—God is well-pleased with them, and they are well-pleased with Him, and He has prepared for them Gardens throughout which rivers flow, therein to abide forever. That is the supreme triumph.[28]

The second half of the articles outlines the agreements made between the Believers, the Helpers, and the Jewish tribes. These three factions merged to form the *Ummah*, as outlined in article 2 of the constitution. Cole identifies the *Ummah* at this point in 622 as an "ecumenical Believers' movement, in which polytheists and other monotheists could be free to practice their own rituals and beliefs."[29]

Articles 17 through 39 highlight the shared commitment towards mutual dependency and self-defense among the Believers. Each group that signed the constitution was part of the wider collective nation, the *Ummah*, or the united communities and nations of Medina.[30] Some of the agreements in this section state that "the peace of the Muslims is indivisible" and that Medina "shall be a sanctuary for the participants of this agreement."

The Constitution of Medina explicitly stated that the Believers, the Helpers, and the Jewish tribes were equal citizens. Article 20 states: "A Jew, who obeys us [Believers and Helpers] shall enjoy the same right of life protection [as the Believers and Helpers do], so long as [the Believers and Helpers] are not wronged by him."[31] The constitution made it clear that the Medinese Jews had the right to freely and openly practice their faith in Medina. There is no reason to doubt that the Medinese Christians were not granted the same human right. While it is not entirely clear if Christians were present at the negotiations that led to the constitution, Muhammad would have likely included them in the "nation of Believers."[32]

Articles 37 and 38 outline the collective approach to be adopted by the Believers, Helpers, and the Jewish tribes if the Medinese came under attack. Article 44 bound all the parties who agreed to the document "to help one another against any attack on Medina." An attack on one tribe was an attack on the whole Medinese population.[33]

Converting to the Islamic faith, or identifying one's self as "Muslim," was not a requirement to belong to the Medinese nation. Nor did the constitution require polytheists or Jews to formally recognize Muhammad as the "Messenger" or "Prophet of God," although he is referred to as such in the agreement.[34] One can surmise that the Christians of Medina were extended the same kind of right in terms of their freedom of religion. The Qur'an, after all, states: "There is no compulsion in religion" (2:256).

The constitution's position on freedom of religion is quite different from the laws created and implemented by Emperor Justinian (d. 565) of the Byzantine Empire. *Corpus juris civilis*, also known by the modern names "Body of Civil Law, "Code of Justinian," or "Justinian's Code," significantly limited the ability of non-Christians to freely practice their religions within the Byzantine realm. Title 11 of the code determined that pagan temples within the borders of Byzantium were illegal and that the practice of pagan sacrifice was punishable by death. Title 9 of the code declared that all Jews and their leaders who attempted to bring "ex-Jews" back to the Jewish faith were to be sentenced to death. If a dispute emerged between Christians and Jews, it would be handled by the ordinary judges, most of which were Christians, thus raising the question of whether Jews could be granted a free and fair trial in the Byzantine courts. Jews were also commanded to pay an annual tax due from all the synagogues. In summary, the Constitution of Medina differs from the Code of Justinian in that minority religious populations are entitled to the same rights and treatment as the majority religious population.

Sociologists refer to a nation in which all people are equal under the law as a civic nation. Michael Ignatieff defines a civic nation as "a community of equal, rights-bearing citizens, united in patriotic attachment to a shared set of political practices and values."[35] Other sociologists have described a civic nation as envisioning "one people" with a common sense of "we," but not in the sense that "we" derives from a particular ethnicity or religion.[36] Civic nations contrast with ethnic nations, which tend to demarcate the boundary of the nation by ancestry and bloodlines. An ethnic nation is "an exclusive nation because it places emphasis on historical experiences and the resulting phenotypes that outline the boundary of the 'natives.'"[37] Muhammad opposed the ethnic nation.

The Medinese civic nation, however, was short lived. The new union between the Aws and the Khazraj made the old alliances with the Nadir, Qaynuqa, and Qurayza unnecessary while simultaneously making the Arab tribes a powerful majority in Medinese society.[38] The Jewish tribes of Medina also started allying themselves with the Quraysh in Mecca, a partnership that Muhammad and the Believers considered a grave threat to their well-being and to the survival of the Constitution of Medina itself. Several Qur'anic verses are believed to have been revealed by God to Muhammad upon learning about the alliance between some of the Jews of Medina and the Qurayshites of Mecca around 624. The Qur'an (8:58) states:

If you have strong reason to fear treachery from a people (with whom you have a treaty), return it to them (i.e. publicly declare to them, before embarking on any action against them, that you have dissolved the treaty) so that both parties should be informed of its termination. Surely God does not love the treacherous.

Qur'an 8:58 is then followed by the following revelation: "And if they (the enemies) incline to peace, incline to it also, and put your trust in God. Surely He is the All-Hearing, the All-Knowing" (8:61).

The climax of the conflict between the Believers and the Jewish tribes of Medina came after a deadly skirmish between a Muslim woman, a Jewish goldsmith, and a Helper.[39] Following the skirmish, the Qaynuqa, in alliance with the Quraysh of Mecca, launched an unsuccessful uprising against Muhammad's leadership. Ibn Ubayy, the Qaynuqan chief, surrendered to Muhammad and asked that mercy be shown toward the Jewish rebels. The Qur'an provides the following revelation that God provided to Muhammad at this moment: "If you meet them in war, deal with them in such a manner as to deter those behind them (who follow them, and those who will come after them), so that they may reflect and be mindful" (8:57).

The Angel Gabriel's protection

The first major war between the Believers and the Qurayshites is known as the Battle of Badr (624), a turning point for the early *Ummah* that started the six-year war between the Believers and the Helpers of Medina and the Qurayshites of Mecca. The battle took place in the month of March near Badr, a city on the trading caravan route along the coast of the Red Sea in western Arabia.

The battle started after Muhammad ordered a small force of men to capture a Meccan caravan led by Abu Sufyan ibn Harb (d. 652), a well-known enemy of the *Ummah* who was returning south to Mecca after trading in the Levant. Capturing the goods of Abu Sufyan's caravan followed the traditional *gazu* practice. According to Armstrong, the *gazu* was

> an accepted fact of life; it was not inspired by political or personal hatred, but was a kind of national sport, conducted with skill and panache according to clearly defined rules. It was a necessity, a rough-and-ready way of redistributing wealth in a region where there was simply not enough to go around.[40]

Before the battle began, Muhammad is reported to have told a concerned Abu Bakr, his close companion, that the Angel Gabriel, armed on horseback, was prepared to fight with the Medinese army in their battle against the Qurayshites.[41]

The Angel Gabriel once again appeared to Muhammad, but on this occasion, the purpose of Gabriel's presence went beyond communicating God's words to Muhammad, as was the case on Laylat al-Qadr at Mount Hira. The Angel Gabriel is said to have physically defended him and the Believers against the Quraysh. Soldiers of the Medinese army reportedly saw many angels riding on horses, led by Gabriel wearing a yellow turban.

The Quraysh were ultimately routed and forced to flee the battlefield at Badr. The Qur'an offers the following verse on the good tidings brought by the Angel Gabriel:

> Say (O Messenger, to them): "(The Lord of the worlds, my and your Lord, declares): 'Whoever is an enemy to Gabriel (should know that) it is he who brings down the Qur'an on your heart by the leave of God, (not out of his own accord), confirming (the Divine origin of and the truths still contained in) the Revelations prior to it, and (serving as) guidance and glad tidings for the believers.'"

> (Enmity to Gabriel, who does nothing other than what he is commanded to do by God, means enmity to God and to His will). Whoever is an enemy to God and His angels and His Messengers and (so) Gabriel and Michael, (should know that) God is surely an enemy to the unbelievers. (Qur'an 2:97–8)

With the Angel Gabriel's assistance, Muhammad not only defeated a much stronger Qurayshite army, said to be composed of 800 soldiers, but also spared the lives of the Qurayshites who were being held as prisoners of war.

Abu 'Amir, the Medinese Christian, is said to have fought alongside the Qurayshites at the Battle of Badr.[42] He was apparently eager to fight with them because his nephew, 'Abd Allah ibn Ubayy, would have likely been crowned king of Medina had it not been for Muhammad's arrival there in 622.[43]

Scholars have noted that Qur'an 5:51 refers specifically to Christians like Abu 'Amir and the Jewish tribes of Medina who plotted against the Believers. The verse reads:

> O you who believe! Take not the Jews and Christians for friends and allies (in their Judaism and Christianity, and against the believers). Some among them are friends and allies to some others. Whoever among you takes them for friends and allies (in their Judaism and Christianity, and against the believers) will eventually become one of them (and be counted among them in the Hereafter). Surely God does not guide such wrongdoers.

Like all Qur'anic verses, Qur'an 5:51 requires historical context. For the Quraysh, Abu 'Amir's actions, and the discussions between the Believers and the Jews of Medina, were intended to break the agreement of mutual protection as outlined in the Constitution of Medina. The Qurayshites' actions posed an existential threat to the Believers and the Helpers. Qur'an 5:51 was revealed to Muhammad in light of specific Jews and Christians, not to Jews and Christians outright for all eternity.

The Medinese army's victory at Badr meant that the ancient trading caravan routes along the Red Sea were no longer accessible to the Qurayshites, who typically traveled northward to trade in the Levant. Abu Sufyan, the commander of the Qurayshite army, considered the blockade an act of war. The Quraysh responded by planning an invasion of Medina. At this time, Muhammad decided against remaining inside the Medinese walls, so he met the Qurayshite army on a strip of cultivated land in the plain below Mount Uhud, which overlooks Medina from the north.[44]

The Battle of Uhud (625) marks Muhammad's first pre-emptive fight against the Qurayshites. Before the war started, Abu Sufyan approached the Medinese army and called on the Aws and Khazraj to switch sides and join the Qurayshites. The Aws and Khazraj, however, refused to accept Abu Sufyan's invitation. Abu 'Amir was again fighting with the Qurayshites. He is also said to have asked the Aws and Khazraj to abandon Muhammad, but the Helpers refused to do so.

While the Battle of Badr ended in victory for Muhammad, the Battle of Uhud concluded in a stunning defeat. Muhammad himself was seriously wounded. The Medinese army was forced to retreat to the higher ground above the Uhud plain. While only twenty-two Qurayshite soldiers were reported to have been killed (out of around 3,000), the Medinese army is said to have suffered over sixty-five deaths.[45] The Qurayshites were now primed to attack Medina, but they instead decided to return to the safety of their homes in Mecca.

Muhammad, meanwhile, returned to Medina with his defeated army and asked the Nadir for support in his struggle against the Qurayshites. Abu Bakr and Umar, among other companions, joined Muhammad in visiting the Nadir's leaders. The two parties reached an agreement whereby the Nadir would assist the Medinese army.

While visiting the Nadir, the Angel Gabriel (once again) appeared to Muhammad and alerted him to an assassination plot organized by Huyayy ibn Akhtab (d. 628), the Nadir tribal chief. Upon receiving this revelation, Muhammad decided to expel the Nadir from Medina because they had openly violated the Constitution of Medina's stipulation that no signee of the constitution should enter into a pact with the Believers' enemies.

The Nadir, in short, refused to adhere to the Constitution of Medina. Abd-Allah ibn Ubayy (d. 631), a Khazrajite who is said to have become a Believer, reportedly urged the Nadir to disobey Muhammad by staying in Medina.[46] Muhammad considered the Nadir's decision to be an act of war.

The Medinese army was prepared to meet Ibn Huyayy's forces on the battlefield, but after several days of preparations, the Nadir army quickly realized that their Khazrajite and Bedouin allies were not coming to their side. Ibn Huyayy ended up telling Muhammad that the Nadir would relinquish their land in Medina to Muhammad's authority. At this critical time, Muhammad reportedly said to the Nadir: "Leave your land and take with you all that your camels can carry, except your arms and armor." The Nadir are said to have either migrated northward to Jericho or Khaybar, or perhaps as far north as southern Syria.[47]

All the while, the Qurayshites were preparing for their next attack on Medina. The Jewish tribes of Medina, and some of the pagan tribes of the city as well, were glad to hear that the Quraysh were preparing for another invasion.

After learning about the Quraysh's preparations in the early months of 626, Muhammad set out toward Badr with 1,500 men on camels and ten horsemen.[48] The Quraysh army never met the Believers on the battlefield of Badr, so Muhammad returned home to Medina where he enjoyed a month-long peace.

The Battle of the Trench

It was around this time, between one campaign and another, that Muhammad again encountered Salman the Persian. Muhammad is reported to have gifted Salman a piece of gold the size of a hen's egg so that he could buy his own freedom. Salman took Muhammad's gift and became a free man. It was in the Enlightened City where Salman is said to have converted to Islam after visiting Muhammad to seek his counsel and help.[49] Later in his life, Salman is said to have translated the Qur'an into Persian, thus becoming the first person to interpret and translate the Islamic holy text into a language other than Arabic.

The next war, however, was not far away. Around the turn of the new year of 627, the exiled Jews of Nadir, who were now settled farther to the north of Medina, were plotting to recover the land they had forfeited to Muhammad. The Nadir's hopes were centered on the Quraysh's preparations for a decisive final blow to Muhammad and the Believers' army.[50] Lings explains the entanglement between the Believers of Medina, the Nadir of Khaybar, and the Quraysh of Mecca:

> Towards the end of the fifth year of Islam [627] ... these preparations were brought to a head by a secret visit to Mecca of [Ibn] Huyayy and other Jewish leaders from Khaybar. "We are one with you," they said to Abu Sufyan, "that we may extirpate Muhammad." "The dearest of men to us," he replied, "are those who help us against Muhammad." So he and Safwan and other chiefs of Quraysh took the Jews inside [al-Ka'bah], and together they swore a solemn oath to God that they would not fail one another until they had achieved their end and aim. Then it occurred to [the] Quraysh that they should take this opportunity of asking the opinion of Jews about the rights of their conflict with the founder of the new religion. "Men of the Jews," said [Abu Sufyan], "[you] are the people of the first scripture, and [you] have knowledge. Tell us how we stand with regard unto Muhammad. Is our religion the better or his?" They answered: "Your religion is better than his, and [you] are nearer the truth than he is."

The Quraysh's alliance with the Nadir to fight the Believers consisted of 4,000 soldiers in several different divisions that were surrounding Medina. The number of total soldiers and the favorable strategic positions made the Quraysh–Nadir force even more intimidating than its presence at the Battle of Uhud.

The coming war in 627—popularly known as the Battle of the Trench—was named after the trenches that Muhammad's army had built around Medina. Salman the Persian was the originator of the trench-building strategy. Having worked as a slave for the Qurayza, the Jewish tribe of Medina, Salman knew how to achieve such a foundation, which ultimately took him and his helpers six days to construct. Salman became a favorite member of the Believers' camp, as Lings explains:

> Salman ... was an object of admiration, for he was not only very strong and able-bodied but for years he had been used to digging and carrying for the [Qurayza]. "He [does] the work of ten men," they said, and a friendly rivalry started up between them. "Salman is ours," the Believers claimed, in virtue of his having left many homes in search of guidance. "He is one of us," the Helpers retorted; "we have more right to him." But the Prophet said. "Salman is one of us, the people of the House."[51]

With Muhammad's army dug into the trenches, it is said that Ibn Huyayy of the Nadir had traveled from Khaybar to join the Quraysh. With Ibn Huyayy's blessing, Abu Sufyan turned his attention to the Qurayza, whose fortress blocked the approach to Medina from the southeast.[52] The Qurayza ended up joining the Qurayshite army, a decision that effectively meant that the Qurayza had renounced their commitment to the Constitution of Medina, which was viewed by Muhammad as another act of treason.

After a twenty-seven-day siege of Medina, the Believers emerged victorious at the Battle of the Trench. Muhammad then turned his attention to the Qurayza, who had broken the laws of the Constitution of Medina.

One morning before the Believers' army marched toward the Qurayza, Angel Gabriel is said to have once again visited Muhammad:

> Gabriel was splendidly dressed, his turban rich with gold and silver brocade, and a cloth of brocaded velvet was thrown over the saddle of the mule he was riding. "Hast thou laid down thine arms, O Messenger of God?" he said, "The Angels have not laid down their

arms, and I return this moment from pursuing the foe, naught else. Verily God in His might and His majesty commandeth thee, O Muhammad, that thou shouldst go against the sons of Qurayzah. I go to them even now, that I may cause their sources to quake."[53]

Upon reaching the Qurayza, it is said that Muhammad offered to preserve the Qurayzahites' lives and property if they joined the Believers. The Qurayza, however, are reported to have preferred dying to joining. Some of Muhammad's companions offered the Qurayza more leniency, but the Qurayza are said to have resisted. With Muhammad's permission, Sa'd, the judge of the Qurayzahites' case, ruled that the rebels should be killed, their property divided, and the women and children taken captive. About 700 men are said to have been put to death. Sa'd's judgment coincided with Jewish law on the punishment of treason and the response to the belligerents of a besieged city.[54]

Around this time, news had come from Abyssinia of the death of 'Ubayd Allah Ibn Jahsh, Muhammad's cousin and brother-in-law. Ibn Jahsh was said to have been a *hanif* or Christian before entering Islam prior to the first *hijra* to Abyssinia. Not long after migrating to Abyssinia, Ibn Jahsh is said to have reconverted to Christianity.[55] According to Lings, Ibn Jahsh's decision to convert to Christianity bothered his wife Umm Habibah, Abu Sufyan's daughter, who was a Muslim herself.[56]

Around four months after Ibn Jahsh's death, Muhammad sent a message to King Ibn Abjar of Abyssinia asking him to stand proxy for him in order to ratify a marriage between him and the widow.[57] Ibn Abjar is said to have agreed to ratify Muhammad's marriage to Habibah. The Christian king is also reported to have thrown a wedding feast in his palace for Habibah, and all the Muslims were invited.[58] While Muhammad and Ibn Abjar never met in person, they appeared to have had mutual respect for each other.

The Lesser Pilgrimage

The Quraysh, meanwhile, learned about Muhammad's decision to travel to Mecca and gathered to figure out how they would respond. As the guardians of al-Ka'bah, where Muhammad and the Believers hoped to worship, the Quraysh would be violating the laws of the sanctuary if they did not grant them permission to enter. On the other hand, if they allowed the pilgrimage to take place, they would be seen by their neighbors and allies as weak. The Quraysh, to say the least, were in a difficult predicament.

The Believers stopped on their march to Mecca at an open tract of land known as Hudaybiyyah. It was in Hudaybiyyah, located about 9 miles outside Mecca, that Muhammad and the Quraysh agreed to a ceasefire that came to be known as *Salah Al-Hudaybiyyah*, or the Treaty of Hudaybiyyah (628), which declared a ten-year truce between the Believers and the Qurayshites. Part of the treaty allowed the Believers to enter Mecca in the following year, at which point the Quraysh would leave the city to allow the Believers to worship freely for a period of three days.

The Believers, nevertheless, were far from safe in Medina. The Nadir tribe of Khaybar, who were encouraging the Quraysh to attack the Believers, were able to strike Medina if need be. Medina, as Lings points out, "could never know any fullness of peace while Khaybar remained as it was."[59]

The Believers' army, under Muhammad's command, attacked the Nadir and took their fortresses in Khaybar. The chief of the Kinanah, one of the most powerful clans of the Nadir tribe, agreed to forfeit his clan's strongholds to Muhammad. The agreement also made sure that no person at the Kinanah garrison would be put to death or made captive so long as they left Khaybar and their possessions became the property of the Believers.[60]

After his return from Khaybar, Muhammad stayed in Medina for the next nine months. Around one year after agreeing to the Treaty of Hudaybiyyah, the Believers set off for Mecca in accordance with the promise of the Quraysh that Muhammad and his followers should have safe passage to al-Kaʿbah to perform the Lesser Pilgrimage, or *'Umrah* in Arabic, which is said to have taken place over the course of three days in 629.[61]

Muhammad proceeded with 2,000 men (in addition to hundreds more women and children) to visit al-Kaʿbah in Mecca to perform the Lesser Pilgrimage. The Believers took their weapons with them fearing the treachery of the Qurayshites, but they left them with a group of 200 men outside of Mecca. Upon Muhammad's arrival, the Qurayshites vacated Mecca and withdrew to the surrounding hills. The Believers, marching in an orderly single file line and dressed in white garments, with some mounted on camels, entered Mecca unopposed.[62]

Mounted on his camel named Al-Qaswa, Muhammad arrived in al-Kaʿbah, touched the black stone with his staff, and then walked around the structure seven times. Afterward, he rested on Safa, a little hill nearby.[63]

Maria the Copt

After performing the Lesser Pilgrimage, Muhammad returned to Medina, where he is said to have married Maria bint Shamʿun (d. 637), better known as Maria al-Qibityya or "Maria the Copt." Maria was a woman from Alexandria, Egypt, who was reportedly presented to Muhammad as a gift from Al-Muqawqis (d. seventh century), the last Byzantine governor of Alexandria. Al-Tabari recounts the story of Maria's arrival in Medina:

> In this year Hatib [Bin] Abu Balta'ah came back from al-Muqawqis bringing Maria and her sister Sirin, his female mule Duldul, his donkey Ya'fur, and sets of garments. With the two women al-Muqawqis had sent a eunuch, and the latter stayed with them. Hatib had invited them to become Muslims before he arrived with them, and Maria and her sister did so. The Messenger of God, peace and blessings of Allah be upon Him, lodged them with Umm Sulaym [bint] Milhan. Maria

was beautiful. The prophet sent her sister Sirin to Hassan b. Thabit and she bore him 'Abd al-Rahman b. Hassan.

Other sources say that Maria retained her Christian faith for the rest of her life and that she never officially married Muhammad. Maria is reported to have lived in a home near an orchard, several miles away from Muhammad's wives, who lived within the al-Masjid al-Nabawi complex. After arriving at her new orchard, Maria gave birth to a baby boy named Ibrahim (d. 632), the Arabic name for Abraham. Ibrahim, however, died as an infant. Historians say that Muhammad enjoyed carrying Ibrahim around Medina. He would even invite his fellow Medinese citizens to meet him.

Muhammad is also said to have married Safiyya bint Huyayy (d. 670), a Jewish woman, around this time. According to the *shari'ah*, the Arabic term for "Islamic law", Muslims are allowed to marry Christians and Jews without compromising the religion of any of the parties involved.[64] It is generally recognized among *shari'ah* scholars that Muslims are permitted to marry a person from Ahl al-Kitab if they are not idol worshippers.[65] The *shari'ah* is also regarded as discouraging compulsions in matters of faith and advocating for freedom of religion.

Battles with the Byzantines

About three months after his return to Medina from the Lesser Pilgrimage in Mecca, Muhammad sent a small group of men to act as messengers of Islam in Syria. On his way to Busra, it was reported that Al-Harith ibn Umayr, a Believer and emissary of Muhammad, was killed by Sharjil ibn Amir, a clan chief of the Ghassanids, an Arab tribe located near the borders of Syria.[66] The Ghassanids were a mostly Christian nation in Byzantium's sphere of influence.

Byzantine forces were positioned in the Levant around this time. Emperor Heraclius is said to have entered into a peace treaty with Shahrbaraz, the Persian general, in 629. The treaty allowed Byzantium to reoccupy some of the empire's previously lost territories, including those in the Levant. Theodorus (d. 636), Heraclius's brother, was in command of the Byzantine army near Balqa when he made the strategic decision to hire Arab tribes as mercenaries in case a war broke out with Muhammad's army.

Murdering one of Muhammad's diplomats was viewed by the Believers as an act of war. In response to the killing, Muhammad organized his army, led by Zaid, the former Christian Ghassanid, to respond to the death of his diplomat by marching toward Maʿan, a territory in southern Syria. While Muhammad's army was in Maʿan, news reached the Believers' camp that Heraclius had arrived to reinforce the Ghassanids with his Byzantine army, which consisted of over 100,000 soldiers, a number that was likely exaggerated by several early Islamic sources.[67] Muhammad's army is reported to have only numbered around 3,000 soldiers.

Whatever the exact numbers of the Byzantine forces, as Lings remarks

the Muslims could see at a glance that they themselves were vastly outnumbered, on a scale that they had never yet experienced. Nor had any of them witnessed before such military splendor as that of the imperial [Byzantine] squadrons that formed the center of the host, with the Arabs on either flank.[68]

To avoid the overwhelming force of Byzantium, Zaid and the Believers retreated southward to Musharif and then retreated farther to Mu'tah, the site of the Battle of Mu'tah (629) between Muhammad's army and the Byzantine Empire.

First in command of the Believers' army at Mu'tah was Zaid ibn Harithah. Second in command was Ja'far ibn Talib (Muhammad's cousin who led the Believers during the first *hijra* to Abyssinia). Third in command was Abdullah ibn Rawaha (d. 629). All three generals died on the battlefield. Thankfully, for Muhammad, Thabit Ibn al-Arqam (d. 675) rallied the Believers and saved the army from total defeat. Khalid bin Walid, another important military figure, was also able to escape alive. Bin Walid said that the fighting at Mu'tah was so intense that he used nine swords, all of which broke during the battle. Around twelve Believers are suspected of having died at Mu'tah. Some scholars, however, question the total number of losses. Daniel C. Peterson, for instance, points out that the ratio of casualties among Muhammad's generals (Zaid, Ja'far, and Abdullah) was unusually high when compared with the losses of the other nine "ordinary" soldiers.[69]

News of the losses at Mu'tah reached Muhammad while he was inside al-Masjid al-Nabawi. Abdur Rahman bin Samrah (d. 670) informed him of the death of his three generals as well as the nine regular soldiers. The Believers near Muhammad at this time are said to have started mourning the losses of the army. Muhammad, however, tried to console them and lift their spirits.

Christian and Islamic sources differ over Muhammad's motivation for engaging with the Byzantines at Mu'tah. Christian sources typically point to the battle as an example of "Islamic aggression" and Muhammad's desire to conquer new territory for the *Ummah*. The Qur'an, on the other hand, points to the defensive nature of Muhammad's actions:

> And fight in the way of God those who fight you, and do not transgress. For indeed God does not like the transgressors. (Qur'an 2:190)

> A sacred month is retributive for another sacred month, and the inviolate values demand retaliation. So whoever attacks you, attack them in like manner as they attacked you. Nevertheless, fear God and remain within the bounds of piety and righteousness, and know that God is with the God-revering, pious. (Qur'an 2:194)

These two Qur'anic passages "granted permission to the Muslims that they may fight in defense against those who fight against them; however, the condition is that they can only fight against those who are actually fighting them or preparing to do so."[70]

Maulana Wahiduddin Khan echoes these positions in stating that Muhammad abandoned peace only when it had become impossible to stick to it.[71] Put another way, Muhammad "fought only when there was no other way left to him."[72] The Qur'an (22:39–40) provides further justification for defensive warfare:

> The believers against whom war is waged are given permission to fight in response, for they have been wronged. Surely God has full power to help them to victory.

> Those who have been driven from their homeland against all right, for no other reason than they that say, "Our Lord is God." Were it not for God's repelling some people by means of others, monasteries and churches and synagogues and mosques, where God is regularly worshipped and His Name is much mentioned, would surely have been pulled down (with the result that God is no longer worshipped and the earth becomes uninhabitable). God most certainly helps whoever helps His cause. Surely, God is All-Strong, All-Glorious with irresistible might.

In summary, defensive warfare is granted in the Qur'an, but this kind of engagement "must be waged, as all good works are in the Qur'an, *fi sabil illah*, 'in the way of God.' That means that even defensive war must observe moral limits, including a scale proportioned to the attack, not going beyond what is necessary to overcome the attackers."[73]

Heraclius and Muhammad

Around the same time as the Battle of Mu'tah, Emperor Heraclius of Byzantium received the news of the Byzantine victory in Homs over the Persian Empire. Heraclius is said to have marched to Jerusalem to return the True Cross to its original location at the Church of the Holy Sepulcher in Jerusalem,[74] which the Persians had plundered. For Christians, the Church of the Holy Sepulcher marks the spot where Jesus was entombed and resurrected.[75] The spot is so sanctified that dominion over its quadrants is divided among the Armenians, Copts, Greek Orthodox, Roman Catholics, and Syrians.[76] Islamic sources also report that, one night, while Heraclius was sleeping in Jerusalem, he had a dream that the years of Byzantine sovereignty over Palestine and Syria were numbered.[77]

Meanwhile, Abu Sufyan of the Quraysh led a trading caravan to Syria. On their journey, they had stopped to trade in Gaza, where Heraclius's men found them, and from there they were immediately taken to Jerusalem.[78] Abu Sufyan is said to have been taken to Heraclius to discuss Muhammad's character and conduct. Al-Bukhari relates the interaction between Abu Sufyan and Heraclius in the following way:

> [Heraclius] invited [Abu Sufyan and his men] into his court of assembly where surrounding him were the great men of Byzantium. He called them close to him and also called for his interpreter and asked, "Who among you is closest in lineage to this man who claims to be a Prophet (of Allah)?" Abu Sufyan responded, "I am the nearest of him in lineage." Heraclius said to his courtiers, "Bring Abu Sufyan close to me, and bring his companions near and put them behind him." Heraclius then said to his interpreter, "Tell them that I am going to ask him about this man. If he tells me a lie, then you all should repudiate him." He [Abu Sufyan] then continued and said: "By Allah! If I was not ashamed that my companions would expose my lie, I would have certainly lied about him." The first question Heraclius asked Abu Sufyan about Muhammad was (as follows):

> Heraclius: What is his lineage among you?
> Abu Sufyan: [Muhammad] belongs amongst us to a noble lineage.
> Heraclius: Has any one of your people ever said what he says (about prophethood) before him?
> Abu Sufyan: No.
> Heraclius: Do the nobles follow him or the weak ones?
> Abu Sufyan: Mostly it is the weak ones who follow him.

Heraclius: Are his followers on the increase or decrease?

Abu Sufyan: They are on the increase.

Heraclius: After entering his religion, does any of them apostatize by being dissatisfied with it?

Abu Sufyan: No.

Heraclius: Did you accuse him of telling lies before he claimed prophethood?

Abu Sufyan: No.

Heraclius: Does he break promises?

Abu Sufyan: No. Now we are in a time of truce with him, but we do not know as to what he will do with it. Abu Sufyan then said, "I could not add anything (to the conversation) except this sentence."

Heraclius: Have you ever fought him?

Abu Sufyan: Yes.

Heraclius: How did your fight against him turn out?

Abu Sufyan: Battles have interchanged between us; sometimes he would get the better of us and sometimes we of him.

Heraclius: What does he order you to do?

Abu Sufyan: He says, "Worship Allah alone, do not associate anything with Him and abandon what (wrong) your ancestors said." He commands us to pray, speak the truth, be chaste, and maintain ties of kinship.[79]

Heraclius thereafter said: "If what you say is true, then he will soon master this very place where my feet are placed."

Abu Sufyan was unable to convince the Byzantine emperor that Muhammad was a treacherous man.[80] Cole writes that the Muslims at this time were likely allied with Emperor Heraclius and that Muhammad engaged in defensive battles against the Quraysh in places such as Badr and Uhud in western Arabia in order to protect Byzantine churches in the region.[81]

Muhammad's relationship with Heraclius has been the subject of scholarly controversy. A letter Muhammad sent to Heraclius is reported to have read:

Allah's name, I begin with, the utmost Kind, the ever Merciful. (This letter is) From Muhammad, the servant of Allah and His Messenger, to Heraclius, Emperor of the Byzantines. Peace be upon the one who follows guidance. After this, I invite you to Islam. If you accept Islam, you will be safe and Allah will double your reward, but if you turn away, you will also earn the sin of your subjects. And "O People of the Book! Come to a word that is common between us and you, that we will not worship anyone except Allah, and we will not associate any partners with Him, and that none of us will take others as lords except Allah." And if they turn away, then you say: "Bear witness that we are Muslims."

According to Islamic sources, Heraclius responded to Muhammad's letter by writing the following:

To Ahmad, the Messenger of God, announced by Jesus, from Caesar, king of the Ar-Rum. I have received your letter with your ambassador and I testify that you are the messenger of God found in our New Testament. Jesus, son of Mary, announced you. I did ask the Ar-Rum to believe in you but they refused. Had they obeyed, it would have been better for them. I wish I were with you to serve and wash your feet.

Muhammad was reportedly informed of Heraclius's positive reaction to his prophethood, but sources also say that Muhammad commented on his refusal to convert to the Islamic faith: "[Heraclius] recognized the truth, but the wicked and malicious one was stingy with his earthly kingdom and possessions, and preferred this worldly life over his religion." Heraclius is then reported to have responded to Muhammad with the following words:

By God, I wish I could renounce this kingdom and go with you and be the servant of your *amir*, but I am not inclined to leave my present situation in this kingdom ... By God, Christ has ordered us in the New Testament to believe in the *ummi* Prophet; however, prosperity and happiness lead to the prolongation of my self-deceit.

As Nadia Maria El-Cheikh points out, these passages "posit a humbled Heraclius who expresses his recognition, coupled with the utmost respect towards the new prophet, but also a Heraclius who ultimately refuses to submit to the new faith."[82] The Islamic tradition, therefore, "presents Heraclius in the dual role of 'recognizer' and near convert to Islam."[83] His double role as emperor of the Byzantine Empire and leading figure of Christendom nevertheless holds important value in confirming Muhammad's prophethood.

5

GUESTS AND HOSTS

Muslim historians have reported that Muhammad also wrote letters to King Khosrow of Persia, Governor Al-Muqawqis of Alexandria, Governor Ghassan of Syria, King Ibn Abjar of Abyssinia, and King Ibn Sawa of Bahrain. Another letter—written to the Christians of Najran—initiated a Christian-Muslim encounter that has been defined as "an event of major importance in the history of the universal church, because of the vast consequences [it] held for the relationships between Christians and Muslims in later centuries and even for the present Christian-Muslim dialogue."[1]

Najran is an ancient city located around 1,200 miles to the south of Medina. A fifth-century document titled *The Martyrdom of Azqir* traces the arrival of Christianity in Najran to Azqir, a priest who evangelized in the days of Sarahbi'il Dankef, the Himyarite king, whose reign is dated sometime between 455 and 475.[2] Christian missionaries were active among the Arab tribes in other cities like Mine and Ukaz. By the sixth century, Najran was recognized as an important caravan crossroad for the trading of cereals, fruits, leathers, textiles, and vegetables.[3]

Muhammad's encounter with the Christians of Najran is documented by Ibn Hisham, as recorded through Ibn Ishaq. Bishop Abu Harithah ibn 'Alqamah of Najran accepted Muhammad's invitation to visit Medina as outlined in the letter, a part of which reads: "In the name of the Lord of Abraham, Isaac and Jacob ... I invite you to worship God instead of worshipping his creatures, so that you may come out of the guardianship of the creatures of Allah and take place under the guardianship of Allah himself."

The Najranite delegation to Medina is said to have been led by three people. The *'aqib*, or leader, was 'Abd Al-Masih,[4] who served as the delegation's governmental affairs official. Al-Aiham as-Sayyid is believed to have served as the delegation's educational and political officer. Ibn 'Alqamah, the bishop, is said to have been the delegation's top scholar. In total, the Christian delegation of Najran consisted of around sixty students, forty-five scholars, and fifteen assistants (for a total of approximately 120 people).

Al-Masjid al-Nabawi, the Arabic term for the "the Mosque of the Prophet," was the main setting for Muhammad's encounter with the Christians of Najran, which is said to have taken place sometime between 22 and 26 March 630. Muslims consider the Mosque of the Prophet to be the second holiest site within the Islamic tradition. At the time of the Christians of Najran's visit, the mosque served as a community center and place of prayer that symbolized the Islamic ideal of *tawhid*, or "the oneness of God." Armstrong notes that *tawhid* "is not simply an abstract metaphysical affirmation of the singularity of the divine, but, like all Qur'anic teaching, a call to action."[5]

Muhammad had part of the *masjid* reserved for the Ahl as-Suffah, or "the People of the Bench," a term named after the people that congregated at a stone bench located near the colonnade of al-Masjid al-Nabawi. Since the *masjid* was part of his own home, Muhammad and his household felt commanded to welcome the growing number of refugees that were drawn by the message of Islam.[6] The People of the Bench are believed to have been mostly poor farmers or tradesmen who had neither wives nor children. The precise number of the Ahl as-Suffah is not known, but it is estimated that up to seventy people made up its permanent residents, including notable names like Bilal ibn Rabah and Salman al-Farisiy, the former Christian.

Dialogue on Christology

The main part of Muhammad's encounter with the Christians of Najran centered on an interreligious dialogue. Successful dialogue means that the involved parties do not seek to "win" an argument or convert another human being to a particular religion. Successful dialogue also entails active participation in a mutual exchange of ideas.

One particular aspect of the dialogue focused on Christology. The Christians of Najran are reported to have shared their view that Jesus is the Son of God, and thus their belief that Jesus is a divine being, a ruling that was finalized at the Council of Nicaea, and then reaffirmed at the Council of Constantinople (381), the Council of Ephesus, and the Council of Chalcedon (451). Bart D. Ehrman captures the early Christian disputes over Christology:

> In early Christianity the views of Christ go "higher and higher" with the passing of time, as he became increasingly identified as divine. Jesus went from being a potential (human) messiah to being the Son of God exalted to a divine status at his resurrection; to being a pre-existent angelic being who came to earth incarnate as a man; to being the incarnation of the Word of God who existed before all time and through whom the world was created; to being God himself, equal with God the Father and always existent with him.[7]

Ibn Ishaq records that Muhammad responded strongly to the claim that Jesus is the Son of God by countering that Jesus was indeed a prophet, but not divine; that God did not have a son;

that the Trinity was not a pure form of monotheism; that Muhammad would not worship anyone or anything but God; and that the Christians of Najran were incorrectly worshipping the cross and sinning by eating pork. Muhammad's alleged choice of words during this exchange raises one of the most common "Islamic critiques" of Christianity. Muhammad appeared to hold the belief that core Christian doctrines like the Trinity were never believed in the earliest years of Christianity but developed in a later period.[8]

Ibn Kathir reports that Muhammad received additional revelations following the Najranites' visit to al-Masjid al-Nabawi. The Qur'anic verse (3:61) revealed near this time reads as follows:

> After the (true) knowledge has come to you, whoever still disputes with you about him (Jesus), say (in challenging them): "Come, then! Let us summon our sons and your sons, and our women and your women, ourselves and your selves, and then let us pray and invoke God's curse upon those who lie."

Muhammad is said to have invoked a *mubahala*, the Arabic term that translates to "prayer curse," on the Najranites for refusing to accept his teachings about Jesus. Bishop 'Alqamah, nonetheless, is reported to have responded to the *mubahala*: "We think it proper not to curse you. You may order us as you like and we shall obey you and shall make peace with you."

The Qur'an (29:46) provides additional context on how Christians and Muslims should use civility in their encounters: "Be courteous when you [Muslims] argue with the People of the Book. Say: 'We believe in that which has been revealed to us and which was revealed to you. Our God and your God is one. To him we submit.'"

While the Qur'an praises Jesus more than any other prophet, it is also critical of Christians who allegedly break their monotheistic covenant with God by believing in the Trinity. The Qur'an states that:

Assuredly they also have disbelieved who say, "God is the third of the Three," whereas there is no deity save the One God. If they desist not from their saying so, there shall touch those of them who persist in unbelief (and die unbelievers) a painful punishment. (Qur'an 5:73)

The Messiah, son of Mary, was but a Messenger; Messengers had passed away before him; and his mother was an upright one wholly devoted to God; both of them ate food (as do all mortals). Look, how We make the truths clear to them, then look how they are turned away from the truth and make false claims! (Qur'an 5:75)

The Islamic holy text mentions that Muhammad is tasked with warning Christians about their Christological beliefs and encouraging Christians to return to a purer monotheism. Qur'an 46:9 reads:

I am not novelty (either in my person or in the message I have brought) among the Messengers, and (being human) I do not know (unless God informs me) what (will happen in the future in the world and therefore what will) be done to me and to you. I only follow what is revealed to me, and I am only a plain warner.

And Qur'an 4:171 adds:

O People of the Book! Do not go beyond the bounds in your religion, and do not say anything of God but the truth. The Messiah, Jesus son of Mary, was but a Messenger of God, and a Word of His (Power) which He conveyed to Mary, and a spirit from Him. So believe in God (as the One, Unique God), and His Messengers (including Jesus, as Messenger); and do not say: (God is one of) a trinity. Give up (this assertion)—(it is) for your own good (to do so). God is but One God; All-Glorified is He in that He is absolutely above having a son. To Him belongs whatever is in the heavens and whatever is on the earth. And God suffices as the One to be relied on, to Whom affairs should be referred.

According to the Qur'an, Muhammad was not the inventor of a new religion "but only a proclaimer of the ancient truths and a mere human being with no supernatural powers."[9] "I am nothing new among the Messengers," he is reported to have said.

The previous Qur'anic verses are similar to the "primitive Christianity" that existed before the Council of Nicaea. Even after the Council of Nicaea:

> [The] various 'Arianizing' movements believed what Unitarians do today—that Jesus was the highest and greatest of human beings, without being God. Humanists like Thomas Jefferson have held similar views. Is the Qur'an therefore 'anti-Christian?' It is more anti-Nicene. It holds that Trinitarian 'Christians' are not Gospel Christians"[10]

The Christological position held by Thomas Jefferson (d. 1826), a Founding Father of the United States and co-author of the Declaration of Independence, mirrors the position taken by Michael Servetus (d. 1553), the sixteenth-century Spaniard and author of *Christianismi restitutio* (1553) who rejected the doctrine of the Trinity. Servetus was a Unitarian Christian who believed that Muhammad emerged to reform Christianity and remind Christians of the purer form of monotheism as adhered to and practiced by Jesus.

The Najranites pray in the Prophet's mosque

Muhammad's encounter with the Christians of Najran continued after the Christological dialogue. The Christians of Najran asked to leave al-Masjid Al-Nabawi in order to engage in their daily prayers. The Najranites decided to exit the building to pray outdoors on the Medinese streets as a sign of the respect that they had for the Islamic prayer space.

Muhammad, however, had a different idea in mind.

As a sign of the respect that he had for his Christian guests, Muhammad informed the Najranites that they were already present in a House of God and that they were welcome to offer their Christian prayers inside al-Masjid al-Nabawi.

The Christians of Najran accepted his invitation.

Muhammad and the Believers likely witnessed the rituals and heard the Christian prayers of the Najranites inside the *masjid*. At that point in time, the Christians and Muslims were effectively occupying the same space and praying under the same roof for the first time in history. In allowing the Christians to pray inside al-Masjid al-Nabawi, Muhammad was sending a clear message that Christians—even Trinitarians—are free to pray inside a *masjid* if they had no other suitable space to offer their prayers.[11]

Pluralism instead of tolerance

Muhammad's encounter with the Christians of Najran is more than a mere example of religious tolerance, which has been defined as the intentional and principled refraining from interfering with an opposed other (or their behavior) in situations of diversity, where the agent believes they have the power to interfere.[12] The encounter in al-Masjid al-Nabawi follows more closely with the theory of religious pluralism as developed by Diana L. Eck.[13] Eck argues that tolerance is an important public virtue, but that it does not require acknowledgment or knowledge of the Other. Eboo Patel similarly argues argues that while religious tolerance should be preferred over bigotry and violence, it also runs the risk of reproducing old patterns of division that are rooted in cultural and religious illiteracy.[14]

Eck's model for understanding religious pluralism has four elements. The first is that diversity should be recognized as a potentially enriching feature of any given society, and that the energetic engagement with that diversity is preferred because it leads to *'asabiyya*, a sociological concept that translates from Arabic to English to mean "social cohesion" or "social solidarity." *'Asabiyya* was developed by Ibn Khaldun (d. 1406), a Tunisian Muslim and author of *Muqaddimah*, to combat clannism and tribalism in favor of democratic-nationalism and republicanism.

Second, respect should be a fundamental feature of human interactions in any given community, but the active seeking of understanding across lines of social difference is the preferred interaction because it leads to more cultural and religious literacy.

Eck's third element of pluralism is that tolerance should guide cross-cultural experiences and interreligious relations, but the culture of encounter and mutually shared commitments across perceived cultural and religious divides is the preferred course of action because it is (potentially) more constructive and enriching.

And finally, dialogue should occur regularly to bridge the gap in cultural and religious illiteracy. Dialogue should be based on criticism and self-criticism because rigorous conversations break down barriers and walls between communities who are perceived to be at odds with each other.

The covenant with the Christians of Najran

The Christians of Najran's visit to Medina is said to have concluded after three days. Ibn Ishaq reports that 'Alqamah, the bishop of Najran, recognized Muhammad as a prophet. Al-Tabari, on the other hand, reports that the Najranites did not recognize Muhammad as a prophet. Nevertheless, the Christian delegation is reported to have said to Muhammad before leaving for Najran: "O, Abu Al-Qasim, we decided to leave you as you are and you leave us as we are. But send with us a man who can adjudicate on our properties, because we accept you." According to these narrations, the Christians of Najran may have submitted to Muhammad's authority as a statesman and a ruler, but they did not convert to the Islamic faith or engage in anti-Islamic polemics.[15]

Bishop 'Alqamah's recognition of Muhammad as a ruler is documented in the "Covenant of Muhammad with the Christians of Najran" (see appendix 3).[16] Intended as a bilateral agreement,

1. The Ancient City of Buṣrā, Syria.

2. Camel Caravan to Mecca, 1910.

3. The Holy Ka'bah.

4. Syriac Orthodox Monastery of Saint Matthew Overlooking the Nineveh Plain.

5. The Angel Gabriel.

6. Ethiopia-Axum Cathedral—Fresco—Black Madonna.

7. Jerusalem, 2013, Temple Mount Dome of the Rock & Chain.

8. Moses Receiving the Law.

9. Cherub Plaque, Louvre.

10. Badr Council.

11. Saint Arethas of Najrān.

12. Mosque of Prophet Muhammad.

13. Al-Masjid al-Nabawī from Inside.

14. Covenant of Prophet Muhammad.

15. Icon of Mary by Luke the Evangelist.

16. Pilgrims at Arafat.

the covenant has language that is characterized by cooperation and mutual respect.[17] Muhammad's agreement with the Najranites is one of many covenants that the prophet of Islam entered into with the Christians of his time.

The covenant with the Christians of Najran is clear in that it provides protection of the land, livelihood, property, and well-being of the Najranites. Muhammad agreed to the following terms in the agreement:

> I hereby declare that my horsemen, my foot-soldiers, my armies, my resources, and my Muslim partisans will protect the Christians as far away as they may be located, whether they inhabit lands which border my empire, in any region, close or far, in times of peace as much as in times of war.

> I commit myself to support them, to place their persons under my protection, as well as their churches, chapels, oratories, the monasteries of their monks, the residences of their anchorites, wherever they are found, be they in the mountains or the valleys, caves or inhabited regions, in the plains or in the desert.

> I will protect their religion and their Church wherever they are found, be it on earth or at sea, in the West or in the East, with utmost vigilance on my part, the People of my House, and the Muslims as a whole.

> I place them under my protection. I make a pact with them. I commit myself to protect them from any harm or damage; to exempt them from any requisitions or any onerous obligations and to protect them myself, by means of my assistants, my followers and my nation against every enemy who targets me and them.

By agreeing to protect the land, livelihood, property, and well-being of the Christians of Najran, Muhammad made it clear that he would work to assist the community's economic and social progress. Muhammad effectively became an ally of the Christians of Najran, just as King Ibn Abjar became an ally of the Believers during the first *hijra*.

The covenant with the Christians of Najran is even more specific in that it protects the positions held by bishops, monks, and other Christians serving as community leaders. Muhammad pledged to protect the Najranites and keep them safe from any interference:

> It is not permitted to remove a bishop from his bishopric, a monk from his monastic life, or anchorite from his vocation as a hermit. Nor is it permitted to destroy any part of their churches, to take parts of their buildings to construct mosques or the homes of Muslims. Whoever does such a thing will have violated the pact of Allah, disobeyed his Messenger, and become estranged from the Divine Alliance.

As noted, the provisions of the covenant provide similar protections to those afforded the Believers during the first *hijra* to the Christian kingdom of Abyssinia, when Ibn Abjar defended Muhammad's followers from being persecuted by the Qurayshite leaders. In a similar way, the covenant also called on Christians to show hospitality towards the Muslims. The text reads:

> [The Christians of Najran] must host for three days and three nights any Muslims who halt among them, with their animals. They must offer them, wherever they are found, and wherever they are going, the same food with which they live themselves, without, however, being obliged to endure other annoying or onerous burdens.

> If a Muslim needs to hide in one of their homes or oratories, they must grant him hospitality, guide him, help him, and provide him with their food during the entire time he will be among them, making every effort to keep him concealed and to prevent the enemy from finding him, while providing for all of his needs.

The covenant calls on the Christians to use their privileges and resources to provide for (and shelter) the Muslims in their midst. The text reads as if the Believers' needs are secondary to the Muslims' needs. The Christians are required by the covenant to take on the struggles of the Muslims as their own struggles. The active defense of Muslim communities within the realm of Byzantium is a form of allyship that places emphasis on equity and inclusion.

The covenant also raises the issue of the *jizya*, a special "tax" imposed on religious minority populations by an "Islamic state."[18] The *jizya* is referred to in the covenant in the following way: "I [Muhammad] forbid any conquerors of the faith to rule over them during their invasions or to oblige them to pay taxes unless they themselves willingly consent."[19] Muhammad included the *jizya* in all the known covenants, but these documents also clearly state that the tax was not to be implemented if Christian populations were suffering from financial hardship.

The *jizya* is often associated with the *dimmi*, the Arabic term and Islamic concept that refers to members of other religious populations living under Islamic rule. The term is also interpreted to mean "protected person." Anver M. Emon claims that the *shari'ah* enables a set of "*dimmi* rules" that subject Christians to various stipulations "regulating the scope of what modern lawyers would call their freedom and liberty, whether to manifest their religious beliefs or to act in ways contrary to Islamic legal doctrines but in conformity with their own normative traditions."[20] Emon's claims appear to support the "*dimmi* rules" as outlined in the Qur'an (9:29):

> Fight against those from among the People of the Book who (despite being People of the Book) do not believe in God and the Last Day (as they should be believed in), and do not hold as unlawful that which God and His Messenger have decreed to be unlawful, and do not adopt and follow the Religion of truth, until they pay the [*jizya*] (tax of protection and exemption from military service) with a willing hand in a state of submission.

At first glance, this Qur'anic verse calls for oppressing of Jews and Christians, but the historical context helps to provide a deeper understanding of the verse. It is true that this verse from *surah* 9 justifies fighting against Jews and Christians, but only under certain conditions. An "Islamic state" is not allowed to attack Christians who have not attacked the Islamic state, who do not oppress Muslims, and who do not try to convert Muslims to Christianity. Muslims are permitted to defend themselves from Christians if—and only if—one or more of these offenses occur.

The agreements spelled out in the covenant may have been shaped by previous treaties between the emperors of Rome and the Christians living throughout the Roman Empire. The Edict of Galerius (311) granted Christians in Roman-controlled lands the right to privately practice Christianity, a privilege they had not previously been granted by the Roman authorities. Emperor Diocletian (d. 311), however, refused to return to Christians the property that the Roman Empire had previously seized from them. Emperors Constantine and Licinius (d. 324) resolved the issue of the seized Christian property in the Edict of Milan (313), which reads:

> We wish those things that belong justly to others, should not only remain unmolested, but should also when necessary be restored... Whence it is our will, that when thou shalt receive this epistle, if any of those things belonging to the Catholic Church of the Christians in the several cities of other places, are now possessed either by the decurions, or any others, these thou shalt cause immediately to be restored to their churches. Since we have previously determined, that whatsoever, these same churches before possessed, shall be restored to their right.

The Edict of Milan went beyond the Edict of Toleration (311) in that relations between the pagan majority of the Roman Empire and its Christian minority changed from one of hostile neutrality to friendly neutrality and protection. Constantine's decision to enact the status of *religio licita*, the Latin term for "tolerated religion," effectively ended the state-sponsored persecution of Christianity within the Roman Empire. While they may seem like contrasting figures, Constantine and Muhammad are similar in that they both introduced a "new religion" to their peoples, and that they initiated a level of religious tolerance that had not previously been seen in their respective realms.

The authenticity of the covenants

It is worth noting that the covenants, in particular the Covenant with the Christians of Najran, have been disputed by scholars. Hamidullah questioned the covenant's authenticity owing to the lack of supporting evidence in the Qur'an and *ahadith*. Addai Scher, an editor and translator of *The Chronicle of Seert*, concluded that the charter is apocryphal, having been forged by Christians so that Muslims would protect their lives and property. John Andrew Morrow, however, claims that Scher fails to advance any evidence in support of his allegation that the covenant in question is counterfeit.[21]

Ahmed El-Wakil offers perhaps the strongest defense of the covenants' authenticity. He notes that the covenants are a complete body of texts containing accurate and plausible accounts of Muhammad's encounters with Christians.[22] Though scholars dispute some of the covenants' details, there is nevertheless a degree of consistency among these texts. According to the College of Islamic Studies at Hamad Bin Khalifa University, the consistency of the details contained in the covenants suggests that they originate from a common source and that they are textually accurate.[23] While the original covenants do not exist, a number of tests have revealed that the copies are faithful replicas of the original versions.

A new era for Najran

The Covenant with the Christians of Najran promised an environment of peaceful coexistence that contrasted with the experiences of previous generations of Christians living around the southern part of the Arabian Peninsula, where Najran is located.

Najran's history in the years before Muhammad's birth is linked to Emperor Justinian, who ruled Byzantium from 518 to 527. Around 523, the Christians of Abyssinia were establishing new merchant posts by traveling to Yemen, a land then populated by the Himyar, a tribe in the ancient Sabaean kingdom of southwestern Arabia. The Himyarite nation, which was concentrated in the area known as Dhu Raydan on the coast of present-day Yemen, ruled over the southern Arabian Peninsula until around 525. By the sixth century, the Himyarites are said to have been converts to Judaism.

The Himyarite Jews were part of the relatively sizeable Jewish population on the Arabian Peninsula at this time. These Arabic-speaking Jews were also present in the western Arabian towns of Khaybar, Tabuk, Tayma, Yathrib (which later became Medina), and Yemen for generations before the sixth century. These Jewish populations were likely in contact with the Jews of Palestine, and as such they were likely versed in scripture and practiced Jewish traditions.[24]

The arrival of the Christians of Abyssinia, who were allied with Emperor Justinian and Byzantium, angered Dhu Nuwas, the Himyarite Jewish king who is said to have served as the Himyarite ruler as early as 517.[25] According to an account written by John of Ephesus (d. 586), Dhu Nuwas declared that he would persecute Christians living in the Himyarite kingdom because his fellow Jews were persecuted under the Code of Justinian throughout the Byzantine Empire. Around 518, Dhu Nuwas is said to have launched an attack that killed some of the merchants at Zafar, a Christian garrison. Dhu Nuwas also reportedly burned a church there. Zafar (or Dhafar as it is also known) was located around 80 miles from Sana'a, the ancient capital of the Sabaean kingdom, from approximately 110 BCE to 525.

After attacking Zafar, the Himyarites proceeded northward toward Najran. According to 'Irfan Shahid, Dhu Nuwas sent an army of 120,000 soldiers to lay siege to the city, which is said to have lasted for around six months. Simeon of Beth Arsham (d. 540), the Syrian bishop at the time, reports that the battle between the Himyarites and the Christians of Najran resulted in many Christian lives lost. Sabaean inscriptions describing the event noted that the losses of the Christians of Najran amounted to around 1,000 killed, 1,500 taken prisoner, and 10,000 head of cattle seized.

Some of the Christians of Najran, reportedly a small group of about 300 people, are said to have surrendered to Dhu Nuwas under the assurance that their lives would be spared. Bishop Arsham, however, states that Bishop Arsham, however, states that Dhu Nuwas ordered the priests, deacons, and other Christians of Najran. Dhu Nuwas ordered the priests, deacons, and other Christians of Najran (reportedly numbering 2,000 people) to also enter the church.[26] The Himyarites are said to have piled wood around the perimeter of the church structure in order to set it on fire. The church was destroyed, and all of the Christians inside the building were burned alive.

Dhu Nuwas, however, was not done attacking the Christians. For a week, he marched his army throughout the region, killing thousands of Christians, who also suffered terrible tortures because they would not renounce their Christian faith. Dhu Nuwas even dug deep pits and filled them with fire. Anyone who refused to convert to Judaism was thrown into the pit. This massacre of the Christians of Najran is mentioned in the Qur'an (85:4–8):

> Ruined were the people of the ditch, of the fire that kept burning with fuel. When they were seated over it, and were themselves witnesses of what they did to the believers. They detested them for no other reason than that they believed in God, the All-Glorious with irresistible might, the All-Praiseworthy.

Such division and infighting between Jews and Christians is condemned in the Qur'an (2:113):

> The Jews say that Christians have nothing (from God) to be based on, and the Christians say the Jews have nothing (from God) to be based on; yet they (both) recite the Book. So, too, those who have no knowledge (from God) say the like of their word. God will judge between them on the Day of Resurrection concerning what they have been disputing.

The next Qur'anic verse (2:114) criticizes Jews and Christians for resorting to violence:

> Who is more in the wrong than he who bars God's places of worship, so that His Name be not mentioned and invoked in them, and strives to ruin them. Such people might never enter them, save in fear (whether because of their alimentation from the Religion or because they try to destroy them owing to their animosity against God). For them is disgrace in the world, and in the Hereafter a mighty punishment.

Ali Ünal in 2012 noted that Qur'an 2:114 denounces any offenses against places of religious worship and alludes to historical examples such as the Bayt al-Maqdis in Jerusalem being ruined by the Assyrian kings, by King Nebuchadnezzar (d. 562) of Babylon, and by Emperor Titus (d. 81). The same verse also refers to the Muslims being prevented from worshipping in al-Ka'bah. In general, Qur'an 2:114 warns against any attempt to close places of worship or ban people from worshipping in them.

Other sources say that Dhu Nuwas wrote a letter to Kavadh I (d. 531), the Persian king, and Al-Mundhir, the king of the Lakhmids, informing them of his actions against the Christians of Najran. Dhu Nuwas reportedly told these two rulers to treat the Christians within the Persian realms in the same way. According to Salo Wittmayer Baron, Al-Mundhir received Dhu Nuwas's letter around January 519. When Al-Mundhir received the letter, he was negotiating a peace treaty between Al-Hirah and Byzantium with a Byzantine delegation from Constantinople.

The Byzantine-Abyssinian-Najranite alliance

The Himyarites' activity on the Arabian Peninsula was a cause for concern in Constantinople, whose Byzantine leaders learned about Dhu Nuwas's attacks on Christians within Byzantium's sphere of influence. Some Christian refugees from Najran are said to have even reached Constantinople, and around 520, Emperor Justin supported the Abyssinian invasion of Yemen to confront Dhu Nuwas.

Justin chose King Kaleb (d. 540), who ruled Abyssinia from 510 to 540, to recover the Byzantine lands that the Himyarites had conquered. The Byzantine emperor is thought to have supported the Abyssinians because they were Monophysites. Byzantium had sought to accomplish several objectives, including pushing back the Himyarites, spreading Monophysitism instead of Nestorianism, and preventing the Persians from intruding farther on the Arabian Peninsula.[27] The Byzantine–Abyssinian invasion of Yemen is believed to have taken place around 525.

The Abyssinians ultimately defeated the Himyarites and emerged as an influential satellite nation of the Byzantine Empire. The Abyssinians, however, had an internal conflict of their own. Procopius (d. 570), the Byzantine historian, reports that Abyssinia had struggled to maintain its influence over Najran. Abraha, the Abyssinian general who defeated Dhu Nuwas, seized power and started building a nation of his own. He broke from Axum, the Abyssinian capital, and deposed King Kaleb's viceroy Esimiphaios (who also is known as Sumuafa' Ashawa') with the help of local Abyssinians who had settled in Yemen.

In response to this development, King Kaleb of Abyssinia sent his additional troops to confront Abraha, but some of his soldiers are said to have defected and joined Abraha, who promoted Christianity in Yemen until his death.

Abraha proceeded to build a church in Sana'a known as Al-Qalis. Islamic historiographers like Ibn Al-Kalbi, Al-Azraqi, and Al-Tabari claim that Abraha's intention in building Al-Qalis was to divert the pagans from the pilgrimage to Mecca in order to attract them to the church in Sana'a. While sources speak of the luxurious decoration of the edifice, only Al-Tabari refers to Abraha having written both to the Aksumite king and to the Byzantine emperor, seeking the latter's help with the mosaics, craftsmen, and marble needed to complete the building.

After completing the church, Abraha is said to have written a letter to the Abyssinian leadership, declaring: "I have built a church for you, O King, such as has not been built for any king before you. I shall not rest until I have directed the Arabs' pilgrimage to it."[28] Subsequently, men were sent from Mecca to attack the church in revenge for competing with al-Ka'bah of Mecca. Abraha's anger at this is given as the reason for the Yemenite attack on Mecca in 570.[29] Upon learning about the purpose of the new church—to direct Arabs away from al-Ka'bah and toward the Christian church—a Qurayshite leader traveled to the church in Sana'a and vandalized it.

On orders from Axum, Abraha marched to Mecca with an army of around 40,000 soldiers to destroy al-Ka'bah and perhaps even to turn Mecca into a Christian kingdom and satellite city of the Abyssinian Empire. Around the same time, Abraha may have also subjected Yathrib and other parts of Arabia to Christian rule.[30]

Several Meccan tribes, including the Hudhayl, Kinanah, and the Quraysh (Muhammad's ancestral tribe), gathered to plan the defense of al-Ka'bah against Abraha. Abraha is said to have sent Hunatah, a Himyarite who was likely Jewish, to Mecca to tell them that he came only to destroy al-Ka'bah. One member of the Quraysh—Abdul-Muttalib ibn Hashim (Muhammad's grandfather)—is reported to have told Hunatah, "God knows that we do not wish to fight him for we have no power to do so." Ibn Hashim is said to have advised his fellow Meccans to seek refuge in the hills on the outskirts of Mecca.

According to Ibn Ishaq, two miracles took place as Abraha's army approached Mecca. The first was that Abraha's main elephant—Mahmud—refused to enter into Meccan territory. The second is that God sent an army of small birds named 'ababil on Abraha's army, which pelted the soldiers with stones. Abraha and his army were unsuccessful in their mission. In fact, according to the Qur'an, the Abyssinian army never even stepped foot inside Mecca's borders.

After Abraha's passing, his son Masruq Abraha (d. 570) continued to maintain an Abyssinian presence in Yemen, but unlike his father, he reinstituted the tribute payments to Axum. Masruq's rule was eventually contested by his half-brother Ma'd-Karib, who asked Emperor Justinian for assistance to overthrow Masruq. Justinian declined the request, leaving Ma'd-Karib no choice but to reach out to Khosrow I, the Persian king. The two sides entered into an alliance that eventually led to the Abyssinian–Persian wars of the late sixth and early seventh centuries. Khosrow's army traveled to conquer the Abyssinians in Yemen by taking its capital, Sana'a. Following the Siege of Sana'a in 570, the year of Muhammad's birth, the capital fell to the Persians. Soon thereafter, Masruq died, leaving Ma'd-Karib's son, Saif, as the natural heir to the Abyssinian throne.

Two years later, around 572, Emperor Justin II (d. 578) of Byzantium started persecuting the Miaphysites, who were no longer loyal to Byzantium.[31] Meanwhile, Khosrow invaded and conquered Yemen. Persia's victory meant that the Persian Empire now gave preference to Judaism over Christianity in their southern Arabian territory.

But, yet again, internal conflict among the Abyssinians presented obstacles to their continued presence in Yemen. Saif was killed by his fellow Abyssinians in 575, five years after Muhammad's birth. Seizing on Abyssinian divisions, the Persians re-invaded Yemen and eventually became the de facto rulers of southern Arabia.

The Byzantine and Persian influence around the Arabian Peninsula, however, started to wane towards the latter years of Muhammad's life, when the Believers movement could no longer be denied their rightful place among the major cultural, political, religious, and social forces of the Near East. Islam emerged as an antidote to the chaos and strife that had been plaguing the region for decades.

6

SYMBOLS AND SOULS

By 630, the Qurayshite leaders realized that their seventeen-year mission to stop Muhammad and the Believers from actualizing Islam was fruitless. Muhammad and the Believers triumphantly returned to Mecca in the same year. The Qurayshites did not resist Muhammad's arrival in the city. Muhammad, in-turn, did not seek revenge against his fiercest enemies. He ensured that their lives and property were safe under his rule in Mecca.

Muhammad's first task upon returning to Mecca was rededicating al-Ka'bah as a monotheistic temple, in accordance with the original intention of Abraham, the founder of the ancient sanctuary. Lings describes the arrival of Muhammad and the Believers in Mecca in the following way:

> [Muhammad] rode straight to the southeast corner of [al-Ka'bah] and reverently touched the [black stone] with his staff, uttering as he did so a magnification. Those who were near him repeated it, *'Allahu 'akbar, 'Allahu 'akbar*, and it was taken up by all the Muslims in the Mosque and the whole of Mecca resounded with it, until [Muhammad] motioned them to silence with his hand. Then he made the seven rounds of the Holy House ...

The Prophet now turned away from [al-Kaʿbah] towards the idols that surrounded it in a wide circle ... Between these and the House he now rode, repeating the verse of the Revelation: "The Truth hath come and the false hath vanished. Verily the false is ever a vanisher," and pointing at the idols, one by one, with his staff; and each idol, as he pointed at it, fell forward on its face. Having completed the circle he dismounted and prayed at the Station of Abraham, which was at that time adjoining [al-Kaʿbah].[1]

Muhammad gave the following message to the crowd that had gathered at al-Kaʿbah to witness its rededication to the Abrahamic tradition: "O Quraysh, God has taken from you the haughtiness of paganism and its veneration of ancestors. Man springs from Adam and Adam sprang from dust." He is said to have then recited the following verse from the Qur'an (49:13):

O humankind! Surely We have created you from a single (pair of) male and female, and made you into tribes and families so that you may know one another (and so build mutuality and co-operative relationships, not so that you may take pride in your differences of race or social rank, and breed enmities). Surely the noblest, most honorable of you in God's sight is the one best in piety, righteousness, and reverence for God. Surely God is All-Knowing, All-Aware.

The Qur'an (49:13) not only embraces diversity but also challenges readers to find ways to cooperate with other human beings who might not physically look like them, or even believe like them.

After stressing the importance of racial equality in front of the *Ummah*, Muhammad added, "O Quraysh, what do you think that I am about to do with you?" The Qurayshites replied by telling Muhammad that he was a "noble man." Muhammad then said: "No reproach this day shall be on you. May God forgive you; indeed, He is the Most Merciful of the merciful" (Qur'an 12:91).

Rather than taking revenge, Muhammad sought forgiveness, just as Joseph, the biblical figure, forgave his brothers who had sold him into slavery in Egypt.

Rededicating al-Kabah

Muhammad proceeded to remove all forms of decorations, money, and pagan statues from al-Ka'bah. In rededicating the sanctuary, Muhammad is said to have removed a pair of ram's horns from inside its walls.[2] According to legend, these ram's horns belonged to the ram sacrificed by Abraham, who offered his son, Ishmael, in accordance with God's will.[3] In Mecca, God is said to have taken Abraham to the well of Zamzam, upon which he and Ishmael built their monotheistic sanctuary, al-Ka'bah. According to Islamic traditions, the Zamzam well sprang up when the baby Ishmael cried from thirst and the well opened for him.[4]

Abraham set the precedent for Muhammad's rededication of al-Ka'bah. In around 2100 BCE, Abraham is said to have destroyed a set of pagan idols in an attempt to convert the Chaldeans of Ur, the Chaldean capital.[5] Abraham's act of idol-breaking represented his "total surrender to the Will of God—his *islam*—which is illustrated by his willingness to subjugate himself to the Divine Command and sacrifice Ishmael, his son by Hagar, his slave. Indeed, Abraham's *islam* is held up as an example for others to follow."[6]

In the process of removing idols from al-Ka'bah, Muhammad is said to have preserved some of the paintings that his Qurayshite ancestors had permitted at the sanctuary. As the protectors of the ancient shrine, Muhammad's ancestors had welcomed the placement of Christian icons and symbols inside the walls of al-Ka'bah.[7] Lings notes that Muhammad's ancestors were, at the least, tolerant of Christianity. The Qurayshites, after all, were motivated by increasing the multitudes of idols and numbers of gods worshipped at al-Ka'bah.

At this time in 630, Mecca may have had a relatively substantial Christian population.[8] It is possible that Christians even witnessed Muhammad's rededication of al-Ka'bah to monotheism.

Saving Jesus and Mary

During the redication of al-Ka'bah, Muhammad is also reported to have saved an icon or fresco of Jesus and Mary that was located inside al-Ka'bah's walls. Shams al-Din al-Dhahabi (d. 1348) claims that:

> on the day of Mecca's conquest, the Messenger of God [Muhammad] entered the House of God [al-Ka'bah] and commanded [that he be given] a garment. He made it wet with water and commanded that the images [inside al-Ka'bah] be wiped out, but he placed his hands on the image of Jesus and his mother and said: "erase everything except for what is under my hands."

According to Al-Azraqi, the fresco of Jesus and Mary showed her with the baby Jesus in her lap, a type of iconography that would have been popular in Christian communities in the seventh century.[9] Taymaz Tabrizi claims that the tradition of protecting Christian objects can be traced back to the early formative period of Islam, when Muslims revered Christian iconography, particularly icons of Jesus and Mary.[10] Tabrizi argues further that Muhammad saved Jesus and Mary to show that whatever misgivings many Muslims of later generations might have had about tolerating Christian iconography, some Muslims—and perhaps even Muhammad himself—might have even revered the icons of Jesus and Mary.[11] Not only did Muhammad allegedly save the depiction of Jesus and Mary but he also reportedly preserved a painting of an old man, said to be Abraham.[12]

The Jesus and Mary fresco inside al-Ka'bah's walls has been linked to Asma bint Shiqr, who is said to have been a frequent visitor to al-Ka'bah. Bint Shiqr is believed to have been a

Ghassanid Christian.[13] Al-Azraqi reports that she had once viewed the Jesus and Mary fresco and said: "By my father and my mother, you belong to the Arabs." Geoffrey R. D. King claims that Al-Azraqi's narration is an independent confirmation of the identity of the figures spared by Muhammad:

> Whether the figure of Maryam (i.e. Mary) looked Arab, stimulating the Ghassan woman's response, or whether the woman was surprised that the Arabs of the Hijaz had a respected picture of Mary/Maryam in Mecca's holiest shrine is unclear. The Ghassanid woman certainly might be expected to recognize a painting of the Virgin, given the depth of Christian influence among the Ghassan Arabs, whose churches and shrines were scattered across Syria.[14]

It is possible that Bint Shiqr was a Miaphysite. The Kingdom of Ghassan is believed to have broken from the wishes of Emperor Justinian of Byzantium by adopting Miaphysitism after the Council of Chalcedon.[15] In 473, Amorkesos, the Ghassanid chief and a Chalcedonian Christian, is said to have signed a treaty with the Byzantine Empire that would acknowledge Byzantium's presence in Palestine. Bint Shiqr could have also been part of the Jafnid clan of the Ghassanid tribe.

Al-Ka'bah remained in the form it had acquired after Muhammad's return until its walls were set on fire and the building itself demolished by the Umayyad caliphate (*khilafah*), an Islamic dynasty that reigned from 661 to 770. The Ummayyads, as they are known, invaded Mecca in 683 in the early years of the second *fitna*, the Arabic term that is generally interpreted to mean "inner conflict" or "intra-group strife."

Al-Azraqi recorded the events surrounding the rebuilding of al-Ka'bah. Baqum al-Rumi, an immigrant living in Mecca, was a carpenter and an architect commissioned by the Qurayshites to rebuild al-Ka'bah. He is sometimes said to have been the master of the sunken Byzantine boat whose wood was used to rebuild al-Ka'bah and may have been an Abyssinian Christian or Coptic

Christian. Al-Azraqi also details a conversation between Al-Rumi and the Quraysh in which it is noted that al-Ka'bah's ceiling and walls were decorated with pictures of the prophets, trees, angels, and a depiction of Jesus and Mary.

The last encounters with Christians

After Muhammad's return to Mecca, he traveled back to Medina where he stayed for around six months. During his stay there, he sent out several small expeditions, one of which was to inquire about the tribe of Tayy. Ali Ibn abu Talib (d. 661), Muhammad's cousin and son-in-law, was placed in charge of this particular expedition to destroy the shrine of Fuls, the center of idol worship for those of the people of Tayy. Adi, a Christian like his father, the poet Hatim, was the leader of the tribe. Adi escaped Tayy with his immediate family, except for his sister, who was taken captive. When Adi's sister was brought to Medina, she asked Muhammad to set her free. Muhammad is reported to have said to the Believers: "Let her go, for her father loved noble ways, and God likewise loveth them."[16]

Around October 631, the Believers' army and the Byzantine army nearly met in Tabuk, a town near the Gulf of Aqaba that is located around 65 miles south of the southernmost point of Jordan. Muhammad marched there, based on the rumor of an imminent Byzantine invasion of Medina. Upon reaching Tabuk, Muhammad's army realized that the rumors of the danger posed by the Byzantines had been unfounded.[17] The Byzantine army was not even there. Muhammad decided against traveling north to engage with the Byzantines because he realized that his army was in no condition to engage in warfare against a mighty force. He had likely learned his lesson from the Battle of Mu'tah.

Muhammad, nevertheless, made use of his ten or so days in Tabuk by entering into several dialogues with local tribal chieftains, some of whom are likely to have been Christians. Yohanas Ibn Ruba, one of the tribal chiefs living near Tabuk, is reported to have been a prince of the Ayla tribe.

While he was traveling back from Tabuk, Muhammad is reported to have destroyed Masjid al-Dirar, the Arabic phrase for the "Mosque of Dissent." Built in Quba, a small village near Medina, Masjid al-Dirar is thought to have been built by twelve disaffected Helpers on the commands of Abu 'Amir Al-Rahib, the Christian who fought against the Believers at the Battles of Badr and Uhud. Islamic sources claim that Abu 'Amir built the *masjid* to attract dissatisfied Believers who had previously been worshipping at al-Masjid al-Nabawi. The following verses of the Qur'an (9:107–10) are believed to be a revelation in response to Abu 'Amir's construction of the building:

> Some among the hypocrites—who have adopted a mosque out of dissension and unbelief, in order to cause division among the believers, and use as an outpost to collaborate with him who before made war on God and His Messenger—will certainly swear—"We mean nothing but good (in building this mosque)," whereas God bears witness that they are surely liars.

> Do not stand in that mosque to do the Prayer. The mosque that was founded on piety and reverence for God from the very first days (in [Medina]) is worthy that you should stand in it for the Prayer. In it are men who love to be purified (of all spiritual and moral blemishes). God loves those who strive to purify themselves.

> Is he better, who founded his building (religion and personal world) on piety and reverence for God, and the aim to please God, or he who founded his building on the edge of a water-worn, crumbling river-bank, so that it tumbles with him into the Hell-fire? God does not guide wrongdoing people.

Meanwhile, Khalid Al-Walid, Muhammad's general, brought some 400 men to Dumat al-Jandal, to the northeast of Tabuk, along the road to Iraq from Medina. Ukaydir ibn Abdul Malik, the Christian ruler of Dumat al-Jandal and a prince of the Kalb tribe, is said to have been taken prisoner by Khalid, who brought Ukaydir to meet Muhammad in Medina. Ukaydir and Muhammad are said to have made an alliance, and the Christian ruler of Dumat al-Jandal later converted to Islam.[18]

Around this time, Muhammad and the Believers received the news that Ibn Abjar, the Abyssinian king who granted asylum to the Believers during the first *hijra*, had passed away. After leading prayers in al-Masjid al-Nabawi, Muhammad turned to the Believers and told them: "This day a righteous man has died. Therefore arise and pray for your brother [Ibn Abjar]."

Reports later came from Abyssinia that a light was constantly seen shining over the king's grave.[19]

The Farewell Sermon

Muhammad's last public appearance in front of the *Ummah* is popularly referred to as the Farewell Sermon (see appendix 4) or the Last Sermon.[20] The date attributed to the sermon is typically 6 March 632. The sermon was delivered on Mount Arafat in the Uranah Valley near Mecca. Muhammad delivered the sermon during the *hajj*, the Islamic pilgrimage season, in front of the biggest gathering of his life. The Farewell Sermon is recognized as having several key themes, such as the abolition of interest in banking (*riba*), charity (*zakat*), condemnation of racism, gender equality, ritual practices, the sanctity of life, and transcending the state of *jahiliyah*.[21]

After praising God at the beginning of the sermon, Muhammad asked his followers to pay close attention to his final teachings. He proceeded to call on the Believers to look after each other's property and well-being, stating that they had a sacred duty to protect both life and people's belongings.

Muhammad then moved on to the topic of humanity. In addition to condemning the idea of racial superiority, he also explicitly stated that all "races" are equal before God:

All mankind is from Adam and Eve. An Arab has no superiority over a non-Arab, nor does a non-Arab have any superiority over an Arab; white has no superiority over black, nor does a black have any superiority over white; [none have superiority over another] except by piety and good action. Learn that every Muslim is a brother and that the Muslims constitute one brotherhood ... Do not, therefore, do injustice to yourselves. Remember, one day you will appear before God and answer for your deeds. So beware, do not stray from the path of righteousness after I am gone.[22]

Muhammad's focus on racial equality in the Farewell Sermon highlights the importance that he placed on belief and faith instead of blood and genealogy when it comes to fostering a sense of belonging to the *Ummah*.[23] The egalitarian vision of the *Ummah* mirrors the words of Paul the Apostle as recorded in the New Testament (Galatians 3:26–8):

It is through faith that all of you are God's children in union with Christ Jesus. You were baptized into union with Christ, and now you are clothed, so to speak, with the life of Christ himself. So there is no difference between Jews and Gentiles, between slaves and free people, between men and women; you are all one in union with Christ Jesus. If you belong to Christ, then you are the descendants of Abraham and will receive what God has promised.

Like Paul the Apostle's efforts in engaging with the Galatians, Muhammad was ushering in a new era of humanity. Muhammad told the *Ummah* at Mount Arafat that the Believers were entrusted with a new covenant in which human beings were bounded by good action and piety rather than gender or race and ethnicity.

The Farewell Sermon, however, does not explicitly mention of Christians or Christianity. What, then, of the future of Christians in the *Ummah*? Should they, according to Muhammad's authority and guidance, be considered full and equal members of the *Ummah*?

Archeological evidence reveals that many churches continued to exist even during the period of the "Islamic conquest" and that new churches were also built during this time. Christians living under Islamic rule were likely paying the *jizya* to affirm their allegiance to the *Ummah* and their commitment to righteousness. When the *jizya* was collected, it did not go directly to the caliphate but rather to the Islamic treasury to be spent for the "public good."[24]

Meeting Ahl al-Kitab in heaven

Muhammad's health started to deteriorate shortly after giving the Farewell Sermon. He is reported to have visited the graves of the Believers who died fighting alongside him at the Battle of Uhud. The last days of his life were spent under the care of A'ishah, his youngest wife. Muhammad managed to make one last trip to al-Masjid al-Nabawi to witness Abu Bakr, his close friend, lead the Believers in prayer. The prophet of Islam reportedly passed away in A'ishah's arms shortly thereafter. In a *hadith*, A'ishah reports that Muhammad's last words were: "There is no god but God, how difficult it is to surrender the soul."

Muhammad had surrendered his soul to Allah, the Supreme Being of the Islamic tradition and the Arabic term for "God," which Christians also worship. In heaven, Muhammad likely once again encountered some of the Ahl al-Kitab, like King Ibn Abjar and Waraqa Ibn Nawfal. Perhaps, together, they gave thanks to the Creator of the Universe.

APPENDIX 1

QUR'ANIC VERSES RELATED TO JESUS

We gave Jesus the son of Mary clear (signs) and strengthened him with the Holy Spirit (2:87).

We believe in Allah, and the revelation given to us, and to Abraham, Ismail, Isaac, Jacob, and the Tribes, and that given to Moses and Jesus, and that given to (all) prophets from their Lord: We make no difference between one and another of them ...

To Jesus the son of Mary We gave clear (signs) and strengthened him with the Holy Spirit (2:253).

O Mary! Allah giveth thee glad tidings of a Word from Him: his name will be Christ Jesus, the son of Mary, held in honor in this world and the Hereafter and of (the company of) those nearest to Allah (3:45).

[Jesus] shall speak to the people in childhood and in maturity. And he shall be (of the company) of the righteous (3:46).

And in their footsteps We sent Jesus the son of Mary, confirming the Law that had come before him: We sent him the Gospel: therein was guidance and light, and confirmation of the Law that had come before him: a guidance and an admonition to those who fear Allah (5:46).

O Jesus the son of Mary! Recount My favor to thee and to thy mother. Behold! I strengthened thee with the Holy Spirit, so that thou didst speak to the people in childhood and in maturity. Behold! I taught thee the Book and Wisdom, the Law and the Gospel and behold! thou makest out of clay, as it were, the figure of a bird, by My leave, and thou breathest into it and it becometh a bird by My leave, and thou healest those born blind, and the lepers, by My leave. And behold! thou bringest forth the dead by My leave. And behold! I did restrain the Children of Israel from (violence to) thee when thou didst show them the clear Signs, and the unbelievers among them said: "This is nothing but evident magic" (5:110).

He [Jesus] said: "I am indeed a servant of Allah: He hath given me revelation and made me a prophet" (19:30).

[Jesus said]: "And He hath made me blessed wheresoever I be, and hath enjoined on me Prayer and Charity as long as I live" (19:31).

[Jesus said]: "So peace is on me the day I was born, the day that I die, and the day that I shall be raised up to life (again)!" (19:33).

When Jesus came with Clear Signs, he said: "Now have I come to you with Wisdom, and in order to make clear to you some of the (points) on which ye dispute: therefore fear Allah and obey me" (43:63).

We sent after them Jesus the son of Mary, and bestowed on him the Gospel; and We ordained in the hearts of those who followed him Compassion and Mercy (57:27).

APPENDIX 2

THE CONSTITUTION OF MEDINA (622)

The following version of the Constitution of Medina was created by Muhammad Hamidullah, who translated the text based on several historical sources including the works of Ibn Hisham, the *Sira* of Ibn Ishaq, *Kitab-Al-Amwal* by Abu Ubaid, and *Al-Bidayah-wan-Nihaya* by Ibn Kathir. Hamidullah's translation is found in his book *The First Written Constitution of the World: An Important Document of the Prophet's Time* (1975).

A Translation of the Constitution of the City-State of Medina in the Time of the Prophet (صلى الله عليه وسلم)

Hamidullah's note:

I have tried to make the translation very clear so as not to require any marginal notes for its understanding. The clauses have been numbered, to facilitate easy reference. Since this numbering has been agreed upon and is the same in Germany, Holland, Italy and other places, so whenever I have had to differ I have indicated my difference by subdividing the clause into (a), (b), etc., so as not to interfere with the international numbering.

In the name of God, the Beneficent and the Merciful

1. This is a prescript of Muhammad (صلى الله عليه وسلم), the Prophet and Messenger of God (to operate) between the

faithful and the followers of Islam from among the Quraysh and the people of Medina and those who may be under them, may join them and take part in wars in their company.

2. They shall constitute a separate political unit (Ummat [or Ummah]) as distinguished from all the people (of the world).

3. The emigrants from the Quraysh shall be (responsible) for their own ward; and shall pay their blood-money in mutual collaboration and shall secure the release of their own prisoners by paying their ransom from themselves, so that the mutual dealings between the Believers be in accordance with the principles of goodness and justice.

4. And Banu [Tribe] 'Aws shall be responsible for their own ward and shall pay their blood-money in mutual collaboration, and every group shall secure the release of its own prisoners by paying their ransom from themselves so that the dealings between the Believers be in accordance with the principles of goodness and justice.

5. And Banu Al-Harith-ibn-Khazraj shall be responsible for their own ward and shall pay their blood-money in mutual collaboration and every group shall secure the release of its own prisoners by paying their ransom from themselves, so that the dealings between the Believers be in accordance with the principles of goodness and justice.

6. And Banu Sa'ida shall be responsible for their own ward, and shall pay their blood-money in mutual collaboration and every group shall secure the release of its own prisoners by paying their ransom from themselves, so that the dealings between the Believers be in accordance with the principles of goodness and justice.

7. And Banu Jusham shall be responsible for their own ward and shall pay their blood-money in mutual collaboration and every group shall secure the release of its own prisoners by paying their ransom so that the dealings between the Believers be in accordance with the principles of goodness and justice.

8. And Banu an-Najjar shall be responsible for their own ward and shall pay their blood-money in mutual collaboration and every group shall secure the release of its own prisoners by paying their ransom so that the dealings between the Believers be in accordance with the principles of goodness and justice.

9. And Banu 'Amr-ibn-'Awf shall be responsible for their own ward and shall pay their blood-money in mutual collaboration and every group shall secure the release of its own prisoners by paying their ransom, so that the dealings between the Believers be in accordance with the principles of goodness and justice.

10. And Banu-al-Nabit shall be responsible for their own ward and shall pay their blood-money in mutual collaboration and every group shall secure the release of its own prisoners by paying their ransom so that the dealings between the Believers be in accordance with the principles of goodness and justice.

11. And Banu-al-Aws shall be responsible for their own ward and shall pay their blood-money in mutual collaboration and every group shall secure the release of its own prisoners by paying their ransom, so that the dealings between the believers be in accordance with the principles of goodness and justice.

12. (a) And the Believers shall not leave any one, hard-pressed with debts, without affording him some relief, in order that the dealings between the Believers be in accordance with the principles of goodness and justice. (b) Also no Believer shall enter into a contract of clientage with one who is already in such a contract with another Believer.

13. And the hands of pious Believers shall be raised against every such person as rises in rebellion or attempts to acquire anything by force or is guilty of any sin or excess or attempts

to spread mischief among the Believers; their hands shall be raised all together against such a person, even if he be a son to any one of them.

14. And no Believer shall kill another Believer in retaliation for an unbeliever, nor shall he help an unbeliever against a Believer.

15. And the protection of God is one. The humblest of them (Believers) can, by extending his protection to any one, put the obligation on all; and the Believers are brothers to one another as against all the people (of the world).

16. And that those who will obey us among the Jews, will have help and equality. Neither shall they be oppressed nor will any help be given against them.

17. And the peace of the Believers shall be one. If there be any war in the way of God, no Believer shall be under any peace (with the enemy) apart from other Believers, unless it (this peace) be the same and equally binding on all.

18. And all those detachments that will fight on our side will be relieved by turns.

19. And the Believers as a body shall take blood vengeance in the way of God.

20. (a) And undoubtedly pious Believers are the best and in the rightest course. (b) And that no associate (non-Muslim subject) shall give any protection to the life and property of a Qurayshite, nor shall he come in the way of any believer in this matter.

21. And if any one intentionally murders a Believer, and it is proved, he shall be killed in retaliation, unless the heir of the murdered person be satisfied with blood-money. And all Believers shall actually stand for this ordinance and nothing else shall be proper for them to do.

22. And it shall not be lawful for any one, who has agreed to carry out the provisions laid down in this code and has

affixed his faith in God and the Day of Judgment, to give help or protection to any murderer, and if he gives any help or protection to such a person, God's curse and wrath shall be on him on the Day of Resurrection, and no money or compensation shall be accepted from such a person.

23. And that whenever you differ about anything, refer it to God and to Muhammad (صلى الله عليه وسلم).

24. And the Jews shall share with the Believers the expenses of war so long as they fight in conjunction.

25. And the Jews of Banu 'Awf shall be considered as one political community [Ummah] along with the Believers—for the Jews their religion, and for the Muslims theirs, be one client or patron. He, however, who is guilty of oppression or breach of treaty, shall suffer the resultant trouble as also his family, but no one besides.

26. And the Jews of Banu-an-Najjar shall have the same rights as the Jews of Banu 'Awf.

27. And the Jews of Banu-al-Harith shall have the same rights as the Jews of Banu 'Awf.

28. And the Jews of Banu Sa'ida shall have the same rights as the Jews of Banu 'Awf.

29. And the Jews of Banu Jusham shall have the same rights as the Jews of Banu 'Awf.

30. And the Jews of Banu al-Aws shall have the same rights as the Jews of Banu 'Awf.

31. And the Jews of Banu Tha'laba shall have the same rights as the Jews of Banu 'Awf. Of course, whoever is found guilty of oppression or violation of treaty, shall himself suffer the consequent trouble as also his family, but no one besides.

32. And Jafna, who are a branch of the Tha'laba tribe, shall have the same rights as the mother tribes.

33. And Banu-ash-Shutaiba shall have the same rights as the Jews of Banu 'Awf; and they shall be faithful to, and not violators of, treaty.

34. And the *mawlas* (clients) of Tha'laba shall have the same rights as those of the original members of it.

35. And the sub-branches of the Jewish tribes shall have the same rights as the mother tribes.

36. (a) And that none of them shall go out to fight as a soldier of the Muslim army, without the permission of Muhammad (صلى الله عليه وسلم). (b) And no obstruction shall be placed in the way of any one's retaliation for beating or injuries; and whoever sheds blood shall be personally responsible for it as well as his family; or else (i.e., any step beyond this) will be of oppression; and God will be with him who will most faithfully follow this code (*sahifdh*) in action.

37. (a) And the Jews shall bear the burden of their expenses and the Muslims theirs. (b) And if any one fights against the people of this code, their (i.e., of the Jews and Muslims) mutual help shall come into operation, and there shall be friendly counsel and sincere behaviour between them; and faithfulness and no breach of covenant.

38. And the Jews shall be bearing their own expenses so long as they shall be fighting in conjunction with the Believers.

39. And the Valley of Yathrib (Medina) shall be a Haram (sacred place) for the people of this code.

40. The clients (*mawla*) shall have the same treatment as the original persons (i.e., persons accepting clientage). He shall neither be harmed nor shall he himself break the covenant.

41. And no refuge shall be given to any one without the permission of the people of the place (i.e., the refugee shall have no right of giving refuge to others).

42. And that if any murder or quarrel takes place among the people of this code, from which any trouble may be feared, it shall be referred to God and God's Messenger, Muhammad (صلى الله عليه وسلم); and God will be with him who will be most particular about what is written in this code and act on it most faithfully.

43. The Quraysh shall be given no protection nor shall they who help them.

44. And they (i.e., Jews and Muslims) shall have each other's help in the event of any one invading Yathrib.

45. (a) And if they (i.e., the Jews) are invited to any peace, they also shall offer peace and shall be a party to it; and if they invite the Believers to some such affairs, it shall be their (Muslims) duty as well to reciprocate the dealings, excepting that any one makes a religious war. (b) On every group shall rest the responsibility of (repulsing) the enemy from the place which faces its part of the city.

46. And the Jews of the tribe of al-Aws, clients as well as original members, shall have the same rights as the people of this code: and shall behave sincerely and faithfully towards the latter, not perpetrating any breach of covenant. As one shall sow so shall he reap. And God is with him who will most sincerely and faithfully carry out the provisions of this code.

47. And this prescript shall not be of any avail to any oppressor or breaker of covenant. And one shall have security whether one goes out to a campaign or remains in Medina, or else it will be an oppression and breach of covenant. And God is the Protector of him who performs the obligations with faithfulness and care, as also His Messenger Muhammad (صلى الله عليه وسلم).

APPENDIX 3

THE COVENANT OF THE PROPHET MUHAMMAD
WITH THE CHRISTIANS OF NAJRAN (630)

The following text of the Covenant of the Prophet Muhammad with the Monks of Najran was created by the Prophet Muhammad and translated by John Andrew Morrow. The translation is found in *Six Covenants of the Prophet Muhammad with the Christians of His Time: The Primary Documents* (2015), edited by John Andrew Morrow.[1]

In the Name of Allah, the Most Compassionate, the Most Merciful

This document has been provided by Muhammad ibn 'Abd Allah ibn 'Abd al-Muttalib, the Messenger of Allah to all of humanity, who was sent to preach and to warn, who has been entrusted the Trust of Allah among his creatures so that human beings would have no pretext before Allah, after his messengers and manifestation, before this Powerful and Wise-Being.

To Sayyid Ibn Harith ibn Ka'b, his co-religionists, and all those who profess the Christian religion, be they in East or West, in close regions or faraway regions, be they Arabs or foreigners, known or unknown.

This document which has been prepared constitutes an authoritative contract, an authentic certificate established on the basis of convention and justice, as well as inviolable pact.

Whoever abides by this edict, shows his attachments to Islam, will be worthy of the best that Islam has to offer. On the contrary, any man who destroys it, breaks the pact which it contains, alters it, or disobeys my commandments will have violated the pact of Allah, transgresses his alliance, and disdained his treaty. He will merit his malediction, whether he is a sovereign authority or someone else.

I commit myself to an alliance and a pledge with them on behalf of Allah and I place them under the safeguard of His Prophets, His Elect, His Saints, the Muslims and the Believers, the first of them and the last of them. Such is my alliance and pact with them.

I proclaim, once again, the obligations that Allah imposed on the Children of Israel to obey Him, to follow His Law, and to respect His Divine Alliance. I hereby declare that my horsemen, my foot-soldiers, my armies, my resources, and my Muslim partisans will protect the Christians as far away as they may be located, whether they inhabit the lands which border my empire, in any region, close or far, in times of peace as much as in times of war.

I commit myself to support them, to place their persons under my protection, as well as their churches, chapels, oratories, the monasteries of their monks, the residences of their anchorites, wherever they are found, be they in the mountains or the valleys, caves or inhabited regions, in the plains or in the desert.

I will protect their religion and their Church wherever they are found, be it on earth or at sea, in the West or in the East, with utmost vigilance on my part, the People of my House, and the Muslims as a whole.

I place them under my protection. I make a pact with them. I commit myself to protect them from any harm or damage; to exempt them for any requisitions or any onerous obligations and to protect them myself, by means of my assistants, my followers and my nation against every enemy who targets me and them.

Having authority over them, I must govern them, protecting them from all damage and ensuring that nothing happens to them that does not happen to me and my Companions who, along with me, defend the cause of Islam.

I forbid any conquerors of the faith to rule over them during their invasions or to oblige them to pay taxes unless they themselves willingly consent. Never should any Christian be subjected to tyranny or oppression in this matter.

It is not permitted to remove a bishop from his bishopric, a monk from his monastic life. Nor is it permitted to destroy any part of their churches, to take parts of their buildings to construct mosques or the homes of Muslims. Whoever does such a thing will have violated the pact of Allah, disobeyed his Messenger, and become estranged from the Divine Alliance.

It is not permitted to impose a capitation or any kind of tax on monks or bishops nor on any of those who, by devotion, wear woolen clothing or live alone in the mountains or in other regions devoid of human habitation.

Let there be a limit set of four *dirhams* per year that all other Christians who are not clerics, monks, or hermits need to pay. Otherwise, let them provide one outfit of striped material or one embroidered turban from Yemen. This is to help Muslims and contribute to the growth of the Public Treasury. Were cloth difficult for them, they should provide its equivalent price, if they themselves willingly consent.

May the capitation of the Christians who have income, who own land, who engage in an important amount of commerce by land or by sea, who exploit mines for precious stones, gold and silver, who are wealthy, not surpass, as a whole, twelve *dirhams* per year, so long as they are inhabitants of these countries and are residents there.

May nothing similar be demanded of travelers, who are not residents of the country or wayfarers whose country of residence is unknown.

There shall be no land tax with capitation for others than those who own land as with the other occupants of inherited properties over which the ruler has a right. They will pay taxes as other pay them without, however, the charges unjustly exceeding the measure of their means. As for the labor force which the owners spend upon to cultivate these lands, to render them fertile, and to harvest them, they are not to be taxed excessively. Let them pay in the same fashion that was imposed on other similar tributaries.

The men who belong to our alliance will not be obliged to go to war with the Muslims in order to combat their enemies, to attack them, and to seize them. Indeed, the members of the alliance will not engage in war. It is precisely to discharge them of this obligation that this pact has been granted to them as well as to assure them the help and protection on the part of the Muslims. No Christian is to be constrained to provide equipment to a single Muslim, in money, in arms or in horses, in the event of a war in which the Believers attack their enemies, unless they contribute to the cause freely. Whoever does so, and contributes spontaneously, will be the object of praise, reward, and gratitude, and his help will not be forgotten.

No Christian will be made Muslim by force. *And dispute ye not with the People of the Book, except with means better* [Qur'an 29:46]. They must be covered by the wings of mercy. Repel every harm that could reach them wherever they may find themselves and in any country in which they are. If a Christian were to commit a crime or an offense, Muslims must provide him with help, defense, and protection. They should pardon his offense and encourage his victim to reconcile with him, urging him to pardon him or to receive compensation in return.

The Muslims must not abandon the Christians, neglect them, and leave them without help and assistance since I have made this pact with them on behalf of Allah to ensure that whatever good befell Muslims it would befall them as well and that whatever harm befell Muslims would befall them as well. In virtue of this pact, they have obtained inviolable rights to enjoy our protection, to be protected from any infringement of their rights, so that they will be bound to the Muslims both in good and bad fortune.

Christians must not be subjected to suffer, by abuse, on the subject of marriages which they do not desire. Muslims should not take Christian girls in marriage against the will of their parents nor should they oppress their families in the event that they refused their offers of engagement and marriage. Such marriages should not take place without their desire and agreement and without their approval and consent.

If a Muslim takes a Christian woman as a wife, he must respect her beliefs. He will give her freedom to listen to her [clerical] superiors as she desires and to follow the path of her own religion. Whoever, despite this order, forces his wife to act contrary to her religion in any aspect whatsoever he will have broken the alliance of Allah and will enter into open rebellion against the pact of His Messenger and Allah will count him among the impostors.

If the Christians approach you seeking the help and assistance of the Muslims in order to repair their churches and their convents or to arrange matters pertaining to their affairs and religion, these must help and support them. However, they must not do so with the aim of receiving any reward. On the contrary, they should do so to restore that religion, out of faithfulness to the pact of the Messenger of Allah, by pure donation, and as a meritorious act before Allah and His Messenger.

In matters of war between them and their enemies, the Muslims will not employ any Christians as a messenger, scout, guide or spy for any other duty of war. Whoever obliges one of them to do such a thing will harm the rights of Allah, will be a rebel against His Messenger, and will cast himself out of His Alliance. Nothing is permitted to a Muslim [with regard to the Christians] outside of obeying these edicts which Muhammad ibn 'Abd Allah, the Messenger of Allah, has passed in favor of the religion of the Christians.

He is also placing conditions [upon the Christians] and I demand that they promise to fulfill and satisfy them as commands their religion, among which, among other things, none of them may act as a scout, spy, either overtly or covertly, on behalf of an enemy of war, against a Muslim. None of them will shelter the enemies of the Muslims in their homes from which they could await the moment to launch an attack. May these enemies [of the Muslims] never be allowed to halt in their regions, be it in their villages, their oratories, or in any place belonging to their co-religionists. They must not provide any support to the enemies of war of the Muslims by furnishing them with weapons, horses, men, or anything else, nor must they treat them as well. They must host for three days and three nights any Muslims who halt among them, with their animals. They must offer them, wherever they are found, and wherever they are going, the same food with which they live themselves without, however, being obliged to endure other annoying or onerous burdens.

If a Muslim needs to hide in one of their homes or oratories, they must grant him hospitality, guide him help, and provide him with their food during the entire time he will be among them, making every effort to keep him concealed and to prevent the enemy from finding him, while providing for all his needs.

Whoever contravenes or alters the ordinances of this edict will be cast out of the alliance between Allah and His Messenger.

May everyone abide by the treaties and alliances which have been contracted with the monks, and which I have contracted myself, and every other commitment that each prophet has made with his nation, to assure them safeguard and faithful protection, and to serve them as a guarantee.

This must not be violated or altered until the hour of the Resurrection, Allah-willing.

This document, by Muhammad ibn 'Abd Allah which contains the covenant he concluded with the Christians and which includes the conditions imposed upon these latter, has been witnessed by:

'Atiq ibn Abi Quhafah, 'Umar ibn al-Khattab; 'Uthman ibn 'Affan; 'Ali ibn Abi Talib; Abu Dharr; Abu al-Darda'; Abu Hurayrah; 'Abd Allah ibn Mas'ud; al-'Abbas ibn 'Abd al-Muttalib; al-Fadl ibn al-'Abbas; al-Zubayr ibn al-'Awwam; Talhah ibn 'Ubayd Allah; Sa'd ibn Mu'adh; Sa'd ibn al-'Awwam; Talhah ibn 'Ubayd Allah; Sa'd ibn Mu'adh; Sa'd ibn 'Ubadah; Thumamah ibn Qays, Zayd ibn Thabit and his son 'Abd Allah; Hurqus ibn Zuhayr; Zayd ibn Arqam; Usamah ibn Zayd; 'Ammar ibn Mazh'un; Mus'ab ibn Jubayr; Abu al-'Aliyyah; 'Abd Allah ibn 'Amr ibn al-'As; Abu Hudhayfah; Ka'b ibn Malik; Hassan ibn Thabit; Ja'far ibn Abi Talib.

[Written by Mu'awiyya ibn Abi Sufyan]

APPENDIX 4

THE FAREWELL SERMON (632)

The Farewell Sermon (also referred to as the Last Sermon or Final Sermon) of Prophet Muhammad was delivered after the *Ummah* completed the *hajj*, the pilgrimage to Mecca. Ibn Hisham offers the following version of the sermon. It has been translated into English.

The Farewell Sermon

O People, lend me an attentive ear, for I know not whether after this year, I shall ever be amongst you again. Therefore, listen to what I am saying to you very carefully and take these words to those who could not be present here today.

O People, just as you regard this month, this day, this city as Sacred, so regard the life and property of each other as sacred. Return the goods entrusted to you to their rightful owners. Hurt no one so that no one may hurt you. Remember that you will indeed meet your Lord, and that He will indeed reckon your deeds. God has forbidden you to take interest, therefore all interest obligation shall henceforth be waived. Your capital, however, is yours to keep. You will neither inflict nor suffer any inequity. God has judged that there shall be no interest, and that all the interest due to Abbas Ibn Abd'al Muttalib[1] shall henceforth be waived.

Beware of Satan, for the safety of your religion. He has lost all hope that he will ever be able to lead you astray in big things, so beware of following him in small things.

O People, it is true that you have certain rights with regard to your women, but they also have rights over you. Remember that you have taken them as your wives only under a trust from God and with His permission. If they abide by your right then to them belongs the right to be fed and clothed in kindness. Do treat your women well and be kind to them for they are your partners and committed helpers. And it is your right that they do not make friends with any one of whom you do not approve, as well as never to be unchaste.

O People, listen to me in earnest, worship God, perform your five daily prayers, fast during the month of Ramadan, and offer *zakat*. Perform *hajj* if you have the means.

All mankind is from Adam and Eve. An Arab has no superiority over a non-Arab, nor does a non-Arab have any superiority over an Arab; white has no superiority over black, nor does a black have any superiority over white; [none have any superiority over another] except by piety and good action. Learn that every Muslim is a brother to every Muslim and that the Muslims constitute one brotherhood. Nothing shall be legitimate to a Muslim which belongs to a fellow Muslim unless it was given freely and willingly. Do not, therefore, do injustice to yourselves.

Remember, one day you will appear before God and answer for your deeds. So beware, do not stray from the path of righteousness after I am gone.

O People, no prophet or apostle will come after me, and no new faith will be born. Reason well, therefore, O People, and understand the words which I convey to you. I leave behind me two things, the Holy Qur'an and my example, the *Sunnah*, and if you follow these you will never go astray.

All those who listen to me shall pass on my words to others and those to others again; and it may be that the last ones understand my words better than those who listen to me directly. Be my witness, O God, that I have conveyed your message to your people.

"This day I have perfected your religion for you, completed my grace upon you, and have chosen Islam for you as your religion" (Qur'an 5:3).

NOTES

INTRODUCTION

1. All of the passages from the Qur'an referenced in this book were retrieved from Ali Ünal's *The Qur'an (With Annotated Interpretation in Modern English)* published by Tughra Books in 2012.
2. Ali S. Asani, "On Pluralism, Intolerance, and the Qu'ran," *American Scholar* 71 (2002), 52–60.
3. Pope Francis, "For a Culture of Encounter," *L'Osservatore Romano* 38, no. 23 (September 2016); http://www.vatican.va/content/francesco/en/cotidie/2016/documents/papa-francesco-cotidie_20160913_for-a-culture-of-encounter.html (accessed 21 January 2021).
4. US Supreme Court, "Courtroom Friezes: South and North Walls," Supremecourt.gov; https://www.supremecourt.gov/about/northandsouthwalls.pdf (accessed 21 January 2021).
5. The other fifteen lawgivers represented in the US Supreme Court are listed in chronological order by the year of their birth: Menes (*fl.* 3200–3000 BCE), the legendary first pharaoh of the first Egyptian dynasty; Hammurabi (1810–1750 BCE), the sixth king of Babylon and founder of the Babylonian Empire; Moses (1393–1273 BCE), the monotheistic Hebrew lawgiver, prophet, and judge of the Israelites; Solomon (990–931 BCE), the king of Israel and judge; Lycurgus (800–730 BCE), the Spartan legislator of Greece; Solon (640–560 BCE), a lawgiver of Athens, Greece; Draco (650–600 BCE), one of Solon's predecessors in Athens; Confucius (551–479 BCE), the Chinese philosopher; Octavian (63 BCE–14 CE), or Augustus, the first Roman emperor; King John (1166–1216),

the king of England who chartered the *Magna Carta*; Louis IX (1214–70), the King of France who was canonized as Saint Louis; Hugo Grotius (1583–1645), the Dutch scholar, lawyer, and statesman; William Blackstone (1723–80), the English law professor and jurist; John Marshall (1755–1835), the fourth Chief Justice of the US Supreme Court; and Napoleon Bonaparte (1769–1821), the emperor of France.

6. All of the passages from the Bible referenced in this book were retrieved from The Holy Bible (New International Version) published by Cambridge University Press in 2014.

7. Hugh Goddard, *A History of Christian–Muslim Relations* (Edinburgh: Edinburgh University Press, 2000), 19.

8. Omid Safi, *Memories of Muhammad: Why the Prophet Matters* (New York: HarperOne, 2009), 80.

9. Stuart Hall, "Ethnicity: Identity and Difference," *Radical America* 13, no. 4 (1991): 9–20.

1. MONKS AND MERCHANTS

1. Christianity formally arrived in Damascus in 391, when the Byzantines converted the Temple of Jupiter, constructed by the Romans under the reign of Emperor Augustus (d. 14), into a cathedral upon the request of Theodosius (d. 395), the emperor of Byzantium.

2. Barnaby Rogerson, *The Prophet Muhammad: A Biography* (Mahwah, NJ: Hidden Spring, 1993), 63–4.

3. Muhammad was the (only) son of 'Abd Allah bin al-Muttalib (d. 570) and Amina bint Wahb (d. 578), his mother. Al-Muttalib was the son of Abdul al-Muttalib ibn Hashim (d. 578) and Fatimah bint Amr (d. 576). Fatimah belonged to the Makhzum clan, regarded as one of the three most powerful clans in Mecca at the time of Muhammad's birth in 570. Muhammad was briefly raised by Amina, who had entrusted him to Halima bint Abu Dhuayb, a wet nurse from the Sa'id ibn Bakr, a Bedouin tribe. As a boy, Muhammad lived in Mecca with his mother for three years, but when he turned six she took him to visit his relatives in Yathrib (later named Medina), a town located about 280 miles to the north of Mecca. Not long after, Amina fell ill and died in Abwa, a town located around 160 miles northwest of Mecca. Following the

death of his mother, al-Muttalib, Muhammad's grandfather, adopted
Muhammad. The two lived in Mecca, where Muhammad likely attended
local Meccan assemblies with his grandfather. After the passing of his
grandfather, Muhammad was placed into the care of Abu Talib ibn Abd
al-Muttalib (d. 619), his merchant uncle and foster father.

4. Scholars have also reported Bahira's name as Georgius, Nestor, Nicholas,
   or Sergius.

5. Muhammad's encounter with Bahira is documented in the *sira*. The *sira*,
   or *as-Sirah an-Nabawiyyah* in Arabic, are the traditional Muslim biog-
   raphies of Muhammad. Muhammad Ibn Ishaq's *Sirat Rasul-Allah* forms
   the basis of Muhammad's biography. The work of Ibn Ishaq (d. 768)
   was preserved in a number of sources, most notably by Ibn Hisham (d.
   833) and Ibn Jarir Al-Tabari (d. 923). These works and others are referred
   to throughout the book in order to shed light on Muhammad's encounters with the Christians of his time.

6. See Muhammad Imdad Hussain Pirzada, *Bukhari: The Sublime Tradition*
   (Eaton Hall, Retford, Nottinghamshire: Al-Karam Publications, 2019),
   24.

7. Karen Armstrong explains the meaning of *badawah* and *gazu* practices:
   "Nomadic (*badawah*) life was a grim, relentless struggle, because there
   were too many people competing for too few resources. Always hungry,
   perpetually on the brink of starvation, the Bedouin fought endless battles with other tribes for water, pastureland, and grazing rights.
   Consequently the *gazu* (acquisition raid) was essential to the *badawah*
   economy. In times of scarcity, tribesmen would regularly invade the territory of their neighbors in the hope of carrying off camels, cattle, or
   slaves, taking great care to avoid killing anybody, since this could lead
   to a vendetta. Nobody considered this in any way reprehensible." See
   Talk of the Nation, "Armstrong: 'Muhammad; A Prophet of Our Time,'"
   National Public Radio (28 November, 2006); https://www.npr.org/tem-
   plates/story/story.php?storyId=6549530 (accessed 21 January 2021).

8. Perhaps the cloud reminded Bahira of the Hebrews leaving Egypt during the Exodus, in which God is said to have led them through the wil-
   derness for forty years, as explained in Exodus (13:20–2): "After leaving Sukkoth [the Hebrews] camped at Etham on the edge of the desert.

By day the Lord went ahead of them in a pillar of cloud to guide them on their way and by night in a pillar of fire to give them light, so that they could travel by day or night. Neither the pillar of cloud by day nor the pillar of fire by night left its place in front of the people." As a scholar of Christianity, Bahira may have also thought about Moses on Mount Sinai. God is said to have revealed himself through a cloud, which had covered the mountain, as Exodus (24:12–17) describes: "The Lord said to Moses, 'Come up to me on the mountain and stay here, and I will give you the tablets of stone with the law and commandments I have written for their instruction. Then Moses set out with Joshua his aide, and Moses went up to the mountain of God. He said to the elders, 'Wait here for us until we come back to you. Aaron and Hur are with you, and anyone involved in a dispute can go to them.' When Moses went up on the mountain, the cloud covered it, and the glory of the Lord settled on Mount Sinai. For six days the cloud covered the mountain, and on the seventh day the Lord called to Moses from within the cloud. To the Israelites the glory of the Lord looked like a consuming fire on top of the mountain. Then Moses entered the cloud as he went on up the mountain. And he stayed on the mountain forty days and forty nights." Furthermore, Bahira may have also thought about the cloud's similarity to Luke (9:28–35), which records Jesus and the Disciples' encounter with a cloud: "[Jesus] took Peter, John and James with him and went up onto a mountain to pray. As he was praying, the appearance of his face changed, and his clothes became as bright as a flash of lightning. Two men, Moses and Elijah, appeared in a glorious splendor, talking with Jesus. They spoke about his departure, which he was about to bring to fulfillment at Jerusalem. Peter and his companions were very sleepy, but when they became fully awake, they saw his glory and the two men standing with him. As the men were leaving Jesus, Peter said to him, 'Master, it is good for us to be here. Let us put up three shelters—one for you and one for Moses and one for Elijah.' (He did not know what he was saying). While he was speaking, a cloud appeared and covered them, and they were afraid as they entered the cloud. A voice came from the cloud, saying, 'This is my Son, whom I have chosen; listen to him.' When the voice had spoken, they found that Jesus was alone. The Disciples did not tell anyone what they had seen."

9. Muhammad's encounter with Bahira is largely considered to be a hagiographical story that depicts Muhammad in flattering terms. Juan Cole states that hagiographical stories such as Muhammad's encounter with Bahira should be taken with a "grain of salt" (see Juan Cole, *Muhammad: Prophet of Peace amid the Clash of Empires* (New York: Bold Type Books), 96). Similarly, Karen Armstrong claims that Muhammad's encounter with Bahira is merely a legend with "symbolic purpose" (see Karen Armstrong, *Muhammad: A Biography of the Prophet* (New York: HarperOne, 1993), 48).

10. William Montgomery Watt, *Muhammad: Prophet and Statesman* (Oxford: Oxford University, 1961), 1–2.

11. Ibid.

12. The French priest Jacques Paul Migne's book *Patrologia Graeca*, or officially *Patrologiae cursus completus: Series Graeca*, is a collection of edited writings published between 1857 and 1866. The collection, written in Greek, is regarded as the largest ever collection of Christian and secular authors of the early and medieval Christian church.

13. Albert Henry Newman, *A Manual of Church History (Volume 1: Ancient and Medieval Church History, to A.D. 1517)* (Philadelphia: American Baptist Publication Society, 1900), 327.

14. Mustafa Akyol, *The Islamic Jesus: How the King of the Jews Became a Prophet of the Muslim* (New York: St. Martin's Press, 2017), 7.

15. Joseph T. Lienhard, "The 'Arian' Controversy: Some Categories Reconsidered," *Theological Studies* 48 (1987): 415–37.

16. The Council of Nicaea was named after the town near the Bosporus Straits. Around 300 bishops and deacons across Christendom attended the council.

17. The Quraysh tribes, whose members are referred to as Qurayshites, are the Arab tribes that served as the custodians of al-Kaʿbah. Muhammad was born into the Hashemite clan of the Quraysh. The Hashimites are named after Hashim ibn ʿAbd Manaf, Muhammad's great-grandfather. The Quraysh ruled Mecca at the time of Muhammad's birth, as the tribe had done for several generations. In the early sixth century, a man of the Quraysh named Qusayy (d. 480) married a daughter of Hulal, who was then the chief of the Khuza'ah. After defeating his rival Hulal in battle, Qusayy became the Meccan ruler and the guardian of al-Kaʿbah.

18. The Abyssinians adopted Christianity as the official state religion as early as the reign of King Ezana (d. 360) sometime between 324 and 328. King Ezana is said to have been influenced by Frumentius, the founder and patron of the Church of Abyssinia. Frumentius was consecrated as the first bishop of the Abyssinian Church in approximately 347. He was given the Arabic name Abuna Salama, or "Bishop of Peace." While Athanasius of Alexandria (d. 373) was defending Trinitarianism against Arianism at the Council of Nicaea (325), the Byzantine Church wrote to King Ezana around 356, during the reign of Emperor Constantius II (d. 361), trying to persuade him to ask Frumentius to travel to Alexandria and receive the Arian doctrine. The Abyssinian Church seems to have rejected the Byzantine request and instead followed the Church of Alexandria's lead. Before Christianity's arrival, Abyssinia is said to have been populated by Jews and polytheists. Abyssinian sources such as the *Kebra Nagast* (The Glory of Kings, in Ethiopic), a fourteenth-century national epic account of the birth of Menelik, the son of Solomon and Makeda, the queen of Sheba, and the *Fetha Nagast* (Law of the Kings, in Ethiopic), a legal code explaining ancient Ethiopian law, described Abyssinia as a Jewish kingdom. The polytheists of Abyssinia worshipped Greek deities including Ares, Poseidon, and Zeus.

19. Cole, *Muhammad*, 31–2.

20. Jack Finegan, *The Archeology of World Religions: The Background of Primitivism, Zoroastrianism, Hinduism, Jainism, Buddhism, Confucianism, Taoism, Shinto, Islam, and Sikhism* (Princeton: Princeton University Press, 1952), 482–5; 492.

21. Cole, *Muhammad*, 21.

22. Craig Considine, *Islam, Race and Pluralism in the Pakistani Diaspora* (London and New York: Routledge, 2018), 44.

23. Unitarian Universalist Association, "Khadijah, First Woman of Islam," UUA.org, n.d.; https://www.uua.org/re/tapestry/youth/bridges/workshop14/khadijah (accessed 8 August 2020).

24. As Muhammad grew as a young man, he refined his skills as a cross-cultural navigator. He became known in Mecca as "Al-Ameen," the Arabic word for "The Trustworthy," and also as "Al-Sadiq," the Arabic word for "The Truthful One."

25. Ibn Sa'd wrote: "[Khadijah] was in those days, the most distinguished in lineage among the Quraysh, the greatest of them in nobility, and the wealthiest of them. Every member of her clan wanted to marry her if he could, seeking her hand and lavishing her with gifts" (see Ibn Sa'd, *Al-Tabaqat al-Kubra*, 1:131).

26. Martin Lings, *Muhammad: His Life Based on the Earliest Sources* (Rochester, VT: Inner Traditions, 2006), 34.

27. Cole, *Muhammad*, 24.

28. A tree is seen on the first page of Genesis, in the first Psalm of the Old Testament, and on the first page and the last page of Revelation in the New Testament. Jesus, for example, was reportedly killed on a cross made from a tree stripped of its roots and branches, as said in John (15:1–6): "[Jesus said] 'I am the true vine, and my Father is the gardener. He cuts off every branch in me that bears no fruit, while every branch that does bear fruit he prunes so that it will be even more fruitful. You are already clean because of the word I have spoken to you. No branch can bear fruit by itself; it must remain in the vine. Neither can you bear fruit unless you remain in me. I am the vine; you are the branches. If you remain in me and I in you, you will bear much fruit; apart from me you can do nothing. If you do not remain in me, you are like a branch that is thrown away and withers; such branches are picked up, thrown into the fire and burned." Other biblical figures are associated with trees. Noah received the olive branch (Genesis 8:11), Abraham sat under the sacred oaks of Mamre (Genesis 18:1), and Moses stood barefoot in front of the burning bush (Exodus 3:2–5). The tree protecting Muhammad may be seen as God's favor, just as trees had protected previous monotheistic leaders before him.

29. Samuel Noble and Alexander Treiger, "Introduction," in Samuel Noble and Alexander Treiger, eds, *The Orthodox Church in the Arab World, 700–1700: An Anthology of Sources* (De Kalb, IL: Northern Illinois University Press, 2014), 8.

30. Kenneth B. Cragg, *Christians and Muslims: From History to Healing* (Bloomington, IN: iUniverse, Inc., 2011), 45.

31. Rom Landau, *Islam and the Arabs* (New York: Macmillan, 1959), 11–21.

32. Muhammad's immediate family had little wealth to speak of. 'Abdullah,

Muhammad's father, died before Muhammad was even born. At the time of his death, 'Abdullah was too young to have acquired land. He had left his son no more than five camels, a small flock of sheep and goats, and one slave (see Lings, *Muhammad*, 24).

33. Al-Ka'bah is reported to have been consecrated by Isaac's descendants as a holy place. For them, al-Ka'bah counted as one of God's tabernacles. Over the centuries, however, the presence of paganism overtook monotheism. Pagans brought idols and stones to worship at al-Ka'bah. Upon seeing paganism at the holy shrine, Abraham's descendants ceased to worship at the temple created by Abraham.

34. Lings, *Muhammad*, 42.

35. Ibid.

36. Ibid., 43.

37. Ibid.

2. ANGELS AND MYSTICS

1. Thomas Carlyle (d. 1881), the Scottish essayist, wrote that Muhammad was a "silent great soul" and hero who had spoken "from Nature's own heart."

2. Gabriel is first described in the Jewish scripture when he appears in the Book of Daniel (8:15–26). Daniel (d. sixth century BCE), a Jerusalemite, and the Jews were taken into captivity by Nebuchadnezzar and lived in exile in Babylon in the sixth century BCE. In these verses, the Angel Gabriel explains to Daniel the meaning of Daniel's vision of encountering a powerful goat. Gabriel returns again in the Book of Daniel (9:25) to foretell the "Anointed One," a name for the Messiah, who would later (for most Christians) emerge as Jesus. In the New Testament (Luke 1:12), Zechariah, the father of John the Baptist and husband of Elizabeth, is said to have encountered Gabriel and trembled before his revelations at the Temple of Solomon in Jerusalem. Luke (1:29–37) then states that Mary, the mother of Jesus, was: "greatly troubled at [Gabriel's] words and wondered what kind of greeting this might be. But the angel said to her, 'Do not be afraid, Mary; you have found favor with God. You will conceive and give birth to a son, and you are to call him Jesus. He will be great and will be called the Son of the Most High. The Lord

God will give him the throne of his father David, and he will reign over Jacob's descendants forever; his kingdom will never end.' 'How will this be,' Mary asked the angel, 'since I am a virgin?' The angel answered, 'The Holy Spirit will come on you, and the power of the Most High will overshadow you. So the holy one to be born will be called the Son of God. Even Elizabeth your relative is going to have a child in her old age, and she who was said to be unable to conceive is in her sixth month. For no word from God will ever fail.'"

3. Pirzada, *Bukhari*, 17.

4. Talk of the Nation, "Armstrong: 'Muhammad; A Prophet of Our Time," National Public Radio, 28 November 2006; https://www.npr.org/templates/story/story.php?storyId=6549530 (accessed 21 January 2021).

5. Muhammad's encounter with Gabriel is similar to Isaiah (29:11–12), which reads: "The meaning of every prophetic vision will be hidden from you; it will be like a sealed scroll. If you take it to someone who knows how to read and ask him to read it to you, he will say he can't because it is sealed. If you give it to someone who can't read and ask him to read it to you, he will answer that he doesn't know how."

6. Lings, *Muhammad*, 45.

7. Muhammad's illness upon returning home, and Khadijah's covering of him with a blanket, mirrors the Book of Daniel. During a vision in the night, Daniel saw what looked like a human being who approached him. Daniel (7:13–15) reads: "In my vision at night I looked, and there before me was one like a son of man, coming with the clouds of heaven. He approached the Ancient of Days and was led into his presence. He was given authority, glory and sovereign power; all nations and peoples of every language worshipped him. His dominion is an everlasting dominion that will not pass away, and his kingdom is one that will never be destroyed. I, Daniel, was troubled in spirit, and the visions that passed through my mind disturbed me." Also in the Book of Daniel (8), Daniel himself was taken to bed because he had fallen sick, just as Muhammad had done after meeting the Angel Gabriel.

8. Lings, *Muhammad*, 16.

9. While Muhammad is said to have been comforted by Khadijah as well as Ibn Nawfal's acceptance and support, it is worth noting that none of

Muhammad's four uncles showed any inclination to believe in the revelations, as Lings writes: "Abu Talib made no objection to the Islam
of his two sons Ja'far and 'Ali, but for himself he said he was not prepared to forsake the religion of his forefathers; Abbas was evasive and
Hamzah uncomprehending, though both assured [Muhammad] of
their unfailing affection for him personally; but Abu Lahab showed
plainly his conviction that his nephew was self-deceived, if not a
deceiver" (see Lings, *Muhammad*, 52).

10. Lings, *Muhammad*, 45.

11. Akyol, *Islamic Jesus*, 86.

12. The *ahadith* (singular—*hadith*) is the Arabic term that refers to "news,"
    "stories," or "reports" that relate to Muhammad's reported actions,
    advice, and sayings. The *ahadith* is a collection of oral narratives that
    were produced by the early Muslim historians of Islam. As a collec-
    tion of Muhammad's sayings, the *ahadith* also provide details about his
    admonitions, biography, conduct, homilies, and encounters in relation
    to Christians. A single *hadith* is a story that reveals Muhammad's
    approval, disapproval, or silence on a given subject that includes, but
    is not limited to, ethical conduct, eschatology, rituals, and virtues. A
    hadith might be based on the testimony of eyewitnesses to Muhammad's
    life, but others might be based on folklore, idealizations, Islamic apol-
    ogetics, and miraculous stories. Each *hadith* noted in this book was
    chosen based on my personal assessment of its relevance to Muhammad's
    encounters with Christians. Scholars have questioned the authenticity,
    credibility, dependability, transferability, and trustworthiness of
    Muhammad's sayings. The *ahadith* contain contradictions, discrepan-
    cies, and internal complexities. As such, some scholars are concerned
    about the limitations of Muhammad's recorded words, so much so that
    they have called for the *ahadith* to be rejected as a legitimate body of
    knowledge. Fred M. Donner, for example, states that: "Some—per-
    haps many—of the incidents related in these sources are not reliable
    accounts of things that actually happened but rather are legends cre-
    ated by later generations of Muslims to affirm Muhammad's status as
    prophet, to help establish precedents shaping their later Muslim com-
    munity's ritual, social, or legal practices, or simply to fill out poorly

known chapters in the life of their founder, about whom, understandably, later Muslims increasingly wished to know everything ... Other elements of his life story may have been generated to make his biography conform to contemporary expectations of what a true prophet would do ..." (See Fred M. Donner, *Muhammad and the Believers: At the Origins of Islam* (Cambridge, MA: Harvard University Press, 2010), 52). A *hadith* is considered weak if it does not fulfill the conditions of a report that is *sahih*, the Arabic term for "authentic." A number of scholars, however, have noted that simply because a *hadith* was not passed down by a complete chain of narrators does not imply that the recording is inauthentic. This book does not engage in any attempt to confirm or refute the authenticity or credibility of the *ahadith* as a whole. My goal instead is to draw inspiration and symbolism from the content of the sources in which the encounters are documented.

13. Mecca's political infrastructure during the time of *jahiliyah* meant that the Meccans struggled to maintain law and order. Justice was typically administered with an "eye for an eye" mentality. Revenge for wrongdoings was commonplace among the tribes. Caravan raiding, guerilla fighting, and outright war were regular occurrences. Slavery was also an institution among the Arabs.

14. Sidney H. Griffith, "The Gospel in Arabic: An Enquiry into Its Appearance in the First Abbasid Century," *Oriens Christianus* 69 (1985), 126–83, here 166.

15. Hikmet Kachouh, *The Arabic Versions of the Gospels: The Manuscripts and Their Families* (Berlin and Boston: De Gruyter, 2012), 79.

16. Henk G. Stoker and Paul Derengowski, "A Discussion about the Version of the Bible Available to Muhammad," *Die Skriflig/In Luce Verbi* 51, no. 2 (2017); https://indieskriflig.org.za/index.php/skriflig/article/view/2262/4776 (accessed 21 January 2021).

17. Ibid.

18. Kurt Aland and Barbara Aland, *The Text of the New Testament: An Introduction to the Critical Editions and to the Theory and Practice of Modern Textual Criticism* (Grand Rapids, MI: Eerdmans, 1989), 194.

19. Stoker and Derengowski, "Discussion about the Version of the Bible."

20. Mustafa Akyol sheds light on the precise meaning of "Son of God."

He notes that in Jewish texts, "Son of God" was merely "any one whose piety has placed him in a filial relation to God." So the term could be used for angels, Israel itself as a nation, or the King of Israel. In Psalms, for example, we read that God would make David his "first born and highest king of earth," and, in return, David would cry, "You are my father" (Psalms 89:26). In this Jewish context, sonship to God implied "divine favour rather than the sharing of the divine nature." In Greek culture, however, the term "Son of God" would imply nothing but God-the-Son—in the sense that Apollo was the son of Zeus. Jesus in fact refers to himself in the Gospels very rarely as "Son of God," but quite frequently as the "Son of Man," or *bar nasha*. The latter is a Jewish term that appears more than 100 times in the Old Testament, most of them in the Book of Ezekiel, where it is used by God to address the prophet Ezekiel, who is clearly a mortal human being. In this Jewish context, the title "Son of Man" implies not deity, but the quite contrary "mortality, impotence, transientness as against the omnipotence and eternality of God." See Akyol, *Islamic Jesus*, 46.

21. Ibid., 35.

22. The Triune understanding of God, also referred to as the Trinity or Trinitarianism, became the established Christian doctrine of the Church following the Council of Nicaea. The Trinitarian Creed, which is largely attributed to Athanasius of Alexandria (d. 373), laid out the requirements of the Christian faith as Christians knew it in the fourth century.

23. Ibid., 6.

24. James D. Tabor, *The Jesus Dynasty: The Hidden History of Jesus, His Royal Family and the Birth of Christianity* (New York: Simon & Schuster, 2006), 261.

25. Ibid.

26. Joseph A. Fitzmyer, "The Qumran Scrolls, the Ebionites and Their Literature," *Theological Studies* 16, no. 3 (1955): 335–72, here 338.

27. Ibid., 370.

28. Ibid., 336.

29. Sakari Häkkinen, "Ebionites," in Antti Marjanen and Petri Luomanen, eds, *A Companion to Second-Century Christian Heretics* (Leiden: Brill, 2005), 246–78, here 248.

30. Akyol, *Islamic Jesus*, 90.

31. Ibid., 9.

32. Bruce Feiler, *Abraham: A Journey to the Heart of Three Faiths* (New York: HarperCollins, 2009), 115.

33. Marmaduke William Pickthall, *The Life of the Prophet Muhammad: A Brief History* (Beltsville, MD: Amana Publications, 1998), 11–12.

34. Lings, *Muhammad*, 16.

35. Alfred Guillaume, *The Life of Muhammad: A Translation of Ibn Ishaq's Sirat Rasul-Allah* (Oxford: Oxford University Press, 1997), 100.

36. A Monophysite is a Christian who holds that Jesus had only one nature, wholly divine, and not two natures, divine and human. Monophysitism, which originates in the teachings of Eutyches, who denied that Jesus's human nature existed together with his divine nature, was classified as "heretical" by the Council of Chalcedon (451).

37. The Levant consists of the historic areas of Lebanon, Jordan, Palestine, and Syria.

38. Mona Siddiqui, *Christians, Muslims, and Jesus* (New Haven and London: Yale University Press, 2013), 9.

39. Ünal, *Qur'an*, 150.

40. Ibid.

41. Juan Cole, "Muhammad and Islamic Peace Studies: Interview with Juan Cole," Inform Consent, 29 August 2018, https://www.juancole.com/2018/08/muhammad-islamic-interview.html (accessed 8 August 2020).

42. Sebastian Günther, "Muhammad, the Illiterate Prophet: An Islamic Creed in the Qur'an and Qur'anic Exegesis," *Journal of Qur'anic Studies* 4, no. 1 (2002), 1–26, here 1.

43. Maulana Wahiduddin Khan, *The True Jihad: The Concepts of Peace, Tolerance and Non-violence in Islam* (New Delhi: Goodword, 2008), 30.

44. Akyol, *Islamic Jesus*, 62.

45. Feiler, *Abraham*, 167.

46. Garry Wills, *What Jesus Meant* (New York: Penguin Books, 2006), 6.

47. Huston Smith, *Islam: A Concise Introduction* (New York: HarperOne, 2008), 227.

48. Garry Wills, *What the Qur'an Meant and Why It Matters* (New York: Penguin Books, 2017), 6.

49. Riza Hassan, "Modernization, Social Change and Religion: A Case Study of the Islamic Ummah," *Lahore Journal of Policy Studies* 4 (2011), 49–58, here 50.

50. The Arabic term *kafir* is typically considered to be the opposite of a "Believer." *Kafir* derives from the Arabic root word *kfr*, or "ingratitude," which implies a discourteous refusal of something that is offered with great kindness and generosity (see Armstrong, *Muhammad*, 66).

51. The Qur'an's use of "Believers" to denote followers of Muhammad's revelations and teachings mirrors the way that Paul of Tarsus referred to the followers of Jesus when he reportedly said in Galatians (3:6–9): "So also Abraham 'believed God, and it was credited to him as righteousness.' Understand, then, that those who have faith are children of Abraham. Scripture foresaw that God would justify the Gentiles by faith, and announced the gospel in advance to Abraham: 'All nations will be blessed through you.'" So those who rely on faith are blessed along with Abraham, the man of faith.

3. ALLIES AND PROPHETS

1. Lings, *Muhammad*, 100.

2. Ibid., 81.

3. Christianity likely arrived in Abyssinia through Philip the Evangelist (d. 11) in the first century. According to Acts (8:26–40), Philip the Evangelist is said to have baptized an Abyssinian eunuch on the road from Jerusalem to Gaza. The Abyssinian eunuch returned to Abyssinia, where he introduced Jesus to the Abyssinians.

4. The queen of Sheba is a biblical figure who is said to have visited King Solomon of Israel in Jerusalem. Historians have identified her with Abyssinia and Yemen in the southern Arabian Peninsula. The Ark of the Covenant is said to be a golden chest that contained the two stone tablets of the Ten Commandments, which were given to Moses by God at Mount Sinai in Egypt. The Church of Our Lady Mary of Zion is an Orthodox church in Ethiopia located in Axum. The original church is reported to have been built by King Ezana of Abyssinia in the fourth century.

5. Some scholars question whether the safety of the Believers was

Muhammad's only concern at the time of the first *hijra* to Abyssinia. William Montgomery Watt claims that Muhammad encouraged the first *hijra* to gain military support from Ashama Ibn Abjar, the Christian king of Abyssinia. The Abyssinians, Watt noted, would have welcomed an excuse to reclaim their lost dominion in Yemen. Watt adds that Muhammad may have even pushed for the migration to make Abyssinia the center of an alternative trade route that was out of the reach of the Quraysh, who were working to cut off any and all potential trading markets for the emerging *Ummah*. In his book *The Throne of Adulis: Red Sea Wars on the Eve of Islam*, Glen W. Bowersock claims that Muhammad encouraged the first *hijra* because of a clash of empires in 615. According to Bowersock, the Persian Empire's capture of Jerusalem in 614 had likely challenged Muhammad and the Believers because they were neither allies of the Persian Empire nor followers of Zoroastrianism, the official religion of the Persians. Four years later, the Persians conquered Egypt, an important economic region of Byzantium, and in 620 the Persians reached Chalcedon.

6. Feiler, *Abraham*, 48.

7. The Christians of Abyssinia in the seventh century were allied with the Byzantines in their wars against the Persians. Byzantium had interest in Abyssinia for the purposes of proselytization and trading. According to Procopius (d. 570), the Byzantine imperial historian, Emperor Justinian of Byzantium sent orders to initiate a new commercial strategy to combat the rising influence of the Persian Empire in the region. The Persians were active in nearby Yemen and supported the Himyarite kingdom.

8. As Mehdi Hasan has noted, Jesus is referred to by name in as many as twenty-five different Qur'anic verses and six times with the title of "Messiah," or "Christ," depending on the translation of the Qur'an. Jesus is also referred to as the "Messenger," "Prophet" "Spirit [of God]," and "Word [of God]." He is the only prophet in the Qur'an that is given these honorific titles. Moreover, Jesus is considered second only to Muhammad in terms of the importance of the 124,000 prophets recognized by Islam (See Mehdi Hasan, "Jesus: The Muslim Prophet," *New Statesman*, December 2009; https://www.newstatesman.com/religion/2009/12/jesus-islam-muslims-prophet (accessed 21 January 2021)).

9. Robert Todd Wise, "Merely a Line in the Sand: A Model for Christian–Muslim Dialogue," *Reformed Journal*, 1 March 2014; https://reformed-journal.com/merely-a-line-in-the-sand-a-model-for-christian-muslim-dialogue/ (accessed 21 January 2021).

10. Zachary Karabell, *People of the Book: The Forgotten History of Islam and the West* (London: John Murray, 2007), 19–20.

11. Samuel Zinner, *The Gospel of Thomas: In the Light of the Early Jewish, Christian and Islamic Esoteric Trajectories* (London: Matheson Trust, 2011), 101.

12. The Council of Nicaea raised additional questions. How could Jesus be both God and man at the same time? An answer to this question was sought by Constantius, the son of Constantine, who replaced his father on the Byzantine imperial throne. Constantius considered removing the Nicene Creed as the official Christological position of the Universal Church.

13. Scholars and theologians have criticized the Trinity for incorporating religious elements that are similar to polytheism in the fourth century, which was largely based on ancient Greek polytheistic philosophy rather than Jesus's life as recorded in the Gospels. Muhammad 'Ata Ur-Rahim and Ahmad Thomson claimed that the Trinity mirrors the many god viewpoints of the ancient Greeks that Paul of Tarsus had incorporated into the idea that Jesus was an indivisible part of God.

14. Anthony A. Hoekema, *The Four Major Cults: Christian Science, Jehovah's Witnesses, Mormonism, Seventh-Day Adventism* (Grand Rapids, MI: Wm. B. Eerdmans-Lightning Source, 1989), 328.

15. Wills, *What the Qur'an Meant and Why It Matters*, 118–19.

16. Akyol, *Islamic Jesus*, 2.

17. Hasan, "Jesus."

18. Ibid.

19. Joshua Roy Porter, "Muhammad's Journey to Heaven," *Numen* 21, no. 1 (April 1974), 64–80, here 67.

20. These events are documented by Ibn Jarir al-Tabari in *Jami' al-Bayan 'an Ta'wil Ay al-Qur'an* (Cairo: Mustafa al-Babi al-Halabi, 1954).

21. Pirzada, *Bukhari*, 411–14.

22. See appendix 1 for Qur'anic verses that address the Islamic perspective of Jesus.

23. John Kaltner states that the "Qur'an's version [of Joseph] has the same characters as the Bible's, and the two texts share the same outline, with both describing Joseph's brothers abandoning him in a pit, his being taken to Egypt and thrown into prison before rising to a position of authority in Pharaoh's court, and his eventual reunion with his father Jacob and his brothers. As is typical of biblical traditions in the Qur'an, the Islamic text has a brief version of events, and it presents them in a way that supports Islamic belief and theology. The most significant difference between the two accounts is the more active role God plays in the Qur'an as compared to Genesis. The deity is mentioned several times in the biblical account but does not have the level of involvement in the story that is found in the Qur'an. In moments of crisis, the characters in the Qur'anic version rely upon God to come to their assistance. God reassures Joseph, after his brothers throw him into the pit, that he will survive the ordeal and confront them about what they have done. When he receives word of his son's presumed death, Jacob exhibits a level of faith and trust in God that is missing from his biblical counterpart. In the scene where his master's wife attempts to seduce him, Joseph does not succumb to the temptation because God is with him" (See John Kaltner, "Joseph in the Qur'an," Bible Odyssey; https://www.bibleodyssey.org/en/people/related-articles/joseph-in-the-quran (accessed 21 January 2021)).

24. Wills, *What the Qur'an Meant and Why It Matters*, 101.

25. Feiler, *Abraham*, 9.

26. Armstrong, *Muhammad*, 85.

27. Ibid., 85–7.

28. John Baldock, *The Essence of Rumi* (London: Arcturus, 2006), 64.

29. The Jewish population of Jerusalem is said to have benefited from General Shahrbaraz's conquest. He allegedly allowed the Jews to return to their holy sites for the first time in 500 years. Jews are also believed to have been appointed to some of Jerusalem's top leadership positions between 614 and 619.

30. Helena, who was later made a saint by the Christian Church, was allegedly guided by a Jewish man who had been given traditional knowledge on its location. Helena ordered Byzantine troops to dig beneath the site

of a former pagan temple built by Emperor Hadrian of the Roman Empire in the 130s. The cross was reportedly found on that site.

31. Chapter 30 of the Qur'an is titled *Ar-Rum*. The entirety of chapter 30 of the Qur'an, as noted by Ali Ünal, "consoled [the Muslims] by predicting the unexpected victory of the Romans against the Persians only nine years after a great defeat. It also implies the future victory of the Muslims, which was soon to occur" (See Ünal, *Qur'an*, 834). One can imagine that Muhammad and the *Ummah* were perhaps ideologically closer to the Christians of Byzantium than they would have been to the Meccan polytheists or the Zoroastrians of Persia. This Qur'anic *surah* was revealed to Muhammad in the mid-Meccan period.

32. Shortly after the Nicene Creed emerged as the official doctrine of the Universal Church, Emperor Constantine decided to move the Roman Empire's capital from Rome to Byzantium, an ancient Greek fishing village located on the Bosporus. Constantine chose Byzantium as the new capital for several reasons. For starters, it was far-away from the Visigoths of the Rhine and Danube Valley, which had been waging war on Rome for decades. Second, Byzantium was situated on the Golden Horn, a strategically positioned natural harbor. Third, Byzantium was in proximity to the Silk Road trade. Byzantium would later be renamed Constantinople (or Constantine's City) by Emperor Theodosius I (d. 395), also known as Theodosius the Great.

33. Constantine is said to have been baptized in 337 by Eusebius of Nicomedia (d. 341), an Arian priest and the bishop of Berytus in Phoenicia. A close ally and friend to Arius, Eusebius is thought to have signed the Trinitarian confession that emerged out of the Council of Nicaea. Eusebius, however, is said to have signed the confession "with hand only, not heart."

34. John F. Haldon, *Byzantium in the Seventh Century: The Transformation of a Culture* (Cambridge: Cambridge University Press, 1997), 52.

35. Nadia Maria El-Cheikh, "Muhammad and Heraclius: A Study in Legitimacy," *Studia Islamica* 89 (1999), 5–21, here 9.

36. Ibid., 5–21.

37. Ibid., 7.

38. Cole, *Muhammad*, 1.

4. CITIZENS AND REBELS

1. Cole, *Muhammad*, 90.

2. Some scholars believe that the first Arab Jews were Jewish migrants from Jerusalem who migrated to the Arabian Peninsula following the destruction of the Temple of Solomon in Jerusalem in 70 CE. Other historians have claimed that the Jews of Yathrib may have had links to the Himyarite kingdom of Yemen. The Himyarites are said to have followed monotheism and perhaps even Judaism specifically as early as the late fourth century. Procopius, the sixth-century historian, claimed that Iotabe, an island at the entrance to the Gulf of Aqaba, was inhabited by "Hebrews." During the reign of Justinian, the Byzantine emperor, the Hebrews of Iotabe are said to have become subjects of Byzantium.

3. Muhammad's first impression of the Jewish tribes of Medina may have been a natural connection considering that the Qur'an (45:16) defines the Jews as God's chosen people: "We did for sure grant to the Children of Israel the Book, and the authority to judge (by the Book), and Prophethood; and We provided them with pure, wholesome things, and exalted them above all other peoples (of their time)."

4. The Quraysh were like other Meccan polytheists in that they erected stones (*ansab*) and images to honor their many gods. Ibn Ishaq (d. 768), the Islamic historiographer, reported that the Quraysh worshipped Hubal, a god housed in al-Ka'bah, the large cubical black stone, shrine, and sanctuary in the middle of Mecca. Al-Ka'bah was the center of the *hajj*, an annual pilgrimage that typically lasted for several days. Warfare and other forms of hostility were forbidden from the area during the sacred pilgrimage season.

5. The Jewish tribes effectively became clients of the Aws and Khazraj after the revolt. However, the Jewish tribes maintained a degree of autonomy in their communal affairs.

6. Cole, *Muhammad*, 90–1.

7. Yathrib was a desert oasis in which access to adequate food and water was a matter of life or death.

8. Lings, *Muhammad*, 58.

9. Yetkin Yildirim, "The Medina Charter: A Historical Case of Conflict

Resolution," *Islam and Christian–Muslim Relations* 20, no. 4 (2009), 439–50, here 440.

10. Ibid., 442.

11. Yildirim, "Peace and Conflict Resolution in the Medina Charter," *Peace Review: A Journal of Social Justice* 18 (2006), 109–10.

12. Muhammad's only possible direct ancestral tie to the city was Salma Bint Amr, his great-grandmother, who some scholars say was a native of Yathrib. Her ties to the city, however, were likely inconsequential in terms of Muhammad's ability to serve as a neutral mediator in the tribal conflicts. Muhammad is also reported to have visited Yathrib as a young boy with Amina, his mother, where he learned to swim in a pool belonging to the Khazraj, his relatives.

13. The *qiblah* changed only around 624 or 625, when a new revelation told the Believers to turn their bodies toward al-Ka'bah and its surroundings, which later became al-Masjid al-Haram, or "The Forbidden Mosque." The Qur'an says that Mecca was the original home of monotheism, and the previous direction toward Jerusalem had been only a test to reveal the true believers.

14. Cole, *Muhammad*, 97.

15. Muhammad Hamidullah, *The First Written Constitution in the World: An Important Document of the Time of the Holy Prophet* (Lahore: Ashraf Printing Press, 1941).

16. Saba Farès, "Christian Monasticism on the Eve of Islam: Kilwa (Saudi Arabia); New Evidence," *Arabian Archaeology and Epigraphy* 22, no. 2 (2011), 243–52.

17. Historical sources also refer to him as Al-Rahib, Abu Sayfi, and *fihi 'ibada,* the Arabic term for "the worshipper."

18. Ghada Osman, "Pre-Islamic Arab Converts to Christianity in Mecca and Medina: An Investigation into the Arabic Sources," *Muslim World* 95, no. 1 (2005), 67–80, here 71–2.

19. Ahmad Ibn Yahya Al-Baladhuri, *Ansab Al-Ashraf* (Damascus: Dar Al-Yaqza, 1997), 328.

20. Lings, *Muhammad*, 131.

21. Ibid., 125

22. Armstrong, *Muhammad*, 113.

23. Cole, *Muhammad*, 103.

24. The Constitution of Medina is also known as the Medina Charter or the *Ummah* Document.

25. Yildirim, "Medina Charter," 439.

26. Medina is also commonly referred to as Al-Medina al-Nabi, the Arabic term for "City of the Prophet" or the Prophet's City.

27. Considered by secular and religious scholars to be the first written constitution in world history, the Constitution of Medina appears to be an authentic document. Hamidullah states that early Islamic historians like Ibn Abu Khaythama and Ibn Ishaq considered the charter to be an authentic historical document that was put into writing around 100 years after the death of Muhammad (d. 632). Hamidullah also claims that these scholars copied the Constitution of Medina in a word-for-word manner. Other scholars, however, disagree on the precise date of the agreement.

28. Muhammad's tolerance of polytheism is also displayed in his encounter with Al-Walid ibn al-Mughira, a notable Meccan who once told Muhammad, who was standing at al-Kaʻbah, to honor the pagan tradition. Muhammad is believed to have recited to him the following verses of the Qur'anic (109:1–6) passage: "Say: 'O you unbelievers (who obstinately reject faith)! I do not, nor ever will, worship that which you worship. Nor are you those who ever worship what I worship. Nor am I one who do ever worship that which you have ever worshipped. And nor are you those who do and will ever worship what I ever worship. You have your religion (with whatever it will bring you), and I have my religion (with whatever it will bring me).'"

29. Cole, *Muhammad*, 102.

30. The Arabic term *Ummah* has historically been translated to mean "Muslim nation" or "united nations."

31. Muhammad Tahir Ul-Qadri, "The Constitution of Islamic State of Medina: The First Written Constitution of Human History"; http://www.constitutionofmadina.com/wp-content/uploads/2012/02/Constitution-of-Madina_Articles.pdf (accessed 21 January 2021).

32. The Qur'an (2:208) instructs the Believers of Medina at this point in time: "O you who believe! Come in full submission to God, all of you,

(without allowing any discord among you due to worldly reasons), and do not follow in the footsteps of Satan, for indeed he is a manifest enemy to you (seeking to seduce you to rebel against God with glittering promises)." The Islamic holy text also warns: "Do not follow in the footsteps of Satan, for he is an open enemy."

33. Bassam Tibi, *Islam between Culture and Politics* (Houndmills, Basingstoke: Palgrave, 2001), 128–9.

34. Lings, *Muhammad*, 129.

35. Michael Ignatieff, *Blood and Belonging: Journeys into the New Nationalism* (New York: Macmillan, 1995), 6.

36. Craig Considine, *The Humanity of Muhammad: A Christian View* (Clifton, NJ: Blue Dome Press, 2020), 49.

37. Craig Considine, "Religious Pluralism and Civic Rights in a 'Muslim Nation': An Analysis of Prophet Muhammad's Covenants with Christians," *Religions* 7, no. 2 (2016), 1–23, here 13.

38. Lings, *Muhammad*, 130.

39. Ibid., 165.

40. Talk of the Nation, "Armstrong: 'Muhammad; A Prophet of Our Time.'"

41. Lings, *Muhammad*, 149.

42. Clifford E. Bosworth, "Iran and the Arabs Before Islam," in Ehsan Yarshater, ed., *The Cambridge History of Iran* (Cambridge: Cambridge University Press, 1983), 593–612, here 600–1.

43. Osman, "Pre-Islamic Arab Converts," 72–3.

44. Lings, *Muhammad*, 178.

45. Ibid., 194.

46. Ibid., 209.

47. Ibid., 211.

48. Ibid., 214.

49. Ibid., 215.

50. Ibid., 222.

51. Ibid., 224.

52. Ibid., 228.

53. Ibid., 237.

54. Ibid., 240.

55. Ibn Jahsh would have taken *as-sahadah*, the Arabic term signifying the declaration of the Islamic faith. *As-sahadah* is one of the Five Pillars of Islam. The declaration of the Islamic faith is as follows: "I bear witness that there is no deity but God, and I bear witness that Muhammad is the messenger of God."

56. Ibid., 267.

57. Ibid.

58. Ibid.

59. Ibid., 271.

60. Ibid., 275.

61. Ibid., 290.

62. Ibid.

63. Ibid., 291.

64. The Qur'an (5:5) notes: "This day all pure, wholesome things have been made lawful for you. And the food of those who were given the Book before (including the animals they slaughter unless, of course, they invoke the name of any other than God) is lawful for you, just as your food (including the animals you slaughter) is lawful for them. And (lawful for you in marriage) are chaste women from among the believers, and chaste women from among those who were given the Book before, provided that you give them their bridal-due, taking them in honest wedlock, and not in debauchery, nor as secret love-companions. (That is the ordinance regarding your relations with the People of the Book in this world. But know this): Whoever rejects (the true) faith (and rejects following God's way as required by faith), all his works are in vain, and in the Hereafter he will be among the losers."

65. See Qur'an 2:221 and Qur'an 36:6.

66. Lings, *Muhammad*, 297.

67. Walter Emil Kaegi claims that the Byzantine army in the entirety of the seventh century may have totaled 100,000 (see Walter E. Kaegi, *Muslim Expansion and Byzantine Collapse in North Africa* (Cambridge: Cambridge University Press, 2010), 99). The total number of Byzantium's soldiers in the seventh century may have even been 50,000. These numbers make it unlikely the Emperor Heraclius deployed all of his forces to fight a relatively small army like Muhammad's.

68. Lings, *Muhammad*, 298.

69. Daniel C. Peterson, *Muhammad, Prophet of God* (Grand Rapids, MI: William. B. Eerdmans, 2007).

70. Muhammad Imdad Hussain Pirzada, *ISIS: State of Ignorance: A Reflection on Islam and Moderation, Extremism and Terrorism, and the Fitnah of ISIS (Daesh)* (Eaton Hall: Al-Karam, 2015), 13.

71. Khan, *True Jihad*, 16–17.

72. Ibid., 17.

73. Wills, *What the Qur'an Meant and Why It Matters*, 132.

74. Michael Mass, *Readings in Late Antiquity: A Sourcebook*, 2nd edn (London: Routledge, 2010), lxxiii.

75. The Al-Husseini family, whose members happen to be Muslim, have served as the custodians to the Church of the Holy Sepulcher since the time of Al-Nasir Salah Al-Din Yusuf Ibn Ayyub (d. 1193), the sultan of Egypt and Syria who is better known simply as Saladin. Generations of men in the Al-Husseini family have held the only key to unlock the church's doors. Their service at this Christian site has helped to maintain the peace between the conflicting Christians in Jerusalem.

76. Feiler, *Abraham*, 92.

77. Lings, *Muhammad*, 301.

78. Ibid., 301–2.

79. Pirzada, *Bukhari*, 32–3.

80. Lings, *Muhammad*, 302.

81. Cole, *Muhammad*, 3.

82. El-Cheikh, "Muhammad and Heraclius," 13.

83. Ibid., 19.

5. GUESTS AND HOSTS

1. Jan Slomp, "The Meeting of the Prophet Muhammad with Christians from Najran and the Present Muslim–Christian Dialogue," *Al-Mushir* 18 (1976), 227–34, here 231–2.

2. Philip M. Forness, *Preaching Christology in the Roman Near East* (Oxford: Oxford University Press, 2018), 122.

3. The city of Sana'a, the ancient Yemenite capital, also served as a center of Christianity on the Arabian Peninsula. Geoffrey R. D. King discusses

the pre-Islamic presence of Christians in Sana'a in "Some Christian Wall-Mosaics in Pre-Islamic Arabia," *Proceedings of the Seminar for Arabian Studies* 10 (1980), 37–43, here 41. The Al-Qalis (alternatively Al-Qulays and Al-Qullays), a church in Sana'a, is described by early Islamic historians like Al-Azraqi, Ibn Al-Kalbi (d. 819), and Al-Tabari (d. 923) as having bronze doors, colored stones, expensive woods, imported marbles, mosaics, and liberally applied gold and silver leaves.

4. Al-Masih's name translates into English as "Slave of the Messiah [or Jesus]."

5. Armstrong, *Muhammad*, 62.

6. Lings, *Muhammad*, 172.

7. Bart D. Ehrman, *How Jesus Became God: The Exaltation of a Jewish Preacher from Galilee* (New York: HarperCollins, 2015), 345.

8. Michael J. Kruger, "Did the Earliest Christians Really Think Jesus Was God? One Important Example," MichaelJKruger.com, 11 December 2014; https://www.michaeljkruger.com/did-the-earliest-christians-really-think-jesus-was-god-one-important-example/ (accessed 21 January 2021).

9. Akyol, *Islamic Jesus*, 63.

10. Wills, *What the Qur'an Meant and Why It Matters*, 120.

11. There are two similar twenty-first-century examples of Christians and Muslims opening their places of worship for prayer. One example occurred in November 2014 when Pope Francis stood shoulder-to-shoulder and bowed his head in prayer with Rahmi Yaran, the Grand Mufti of Istanbul, inside the seventeenth-century Sultan Ahmet Mosque, also known as the Blue Mosque for the blue tiles that embellish its walls. In that same month and year, Reverend Canon Gina Campbell of the National Cathedral in Washington, DC invited Muslims to use the cathedral for their own prayer services. Despite a lone anti-Islam protestor briefly disrupting the day's event, the encounter proceeded accordingly with the themes of coexistence and humanity.

12. Andrew Jason Cohen, "What Toleration Is," *Ethics* 115, no. 1 (October 2004), 68–95, here 69.

13. Diana L. Eck, "What Is Pluralism?," Harvard Pluralism Project, 2006; http://pluralism.org/what-is-pluralism/ (accessed 22 July 2019).

14. Eboo Patel, *Out of Many Faiths: Religious Diversity and the American Promise* (Princeton: Princeton University Press, 2018).

15. Converting to the Islamic faith requires that a person states the "Islamic creed" or the testimony of faith, known as the *as-sahadah*. The *as-sahadah* states *La ilaha illa-'llah, Muhammadan rasula 'ilah* (There is no god but God, Muhammad is the Messenger of God).

16. John Andrew Morrow, *The Covenants of the Prophet Muhammad with the Christians of the World* (Tacoma: Angelico Press/Sophia Perennis, 2013).

17. Some of the early Islamic works that reference the Covenant with the Christians of Najran include *Al-Tabaqat al-Kubra* by Ibn Sa'd and *Kitab Futuh al-Buldan* by Al-Baladhuri (1916).

18. The *jizya* is a tax that, among other things, guarantees groups like Jews and Christians physical safety, protection of families and property, exemption from serving in the military and fighting in war. Anti-Islam critics use the *jizya* as a means to denigrate Muslims and paint them as a "fifth column" or enemy group.

19. Morrow, *Covenants of the Prophet Muhammad*, 298.

20. Anver M. Emon, "Religious Minorities and Islamic Law: Accommodation and the Limits of Tolerance," in Anver M. Emon, Mark Ellis, and Benjamin Glahn, eds, *Islamic Law and International Human Rights* (Oxford: Oxford University Press, 2012), 323–43, here 323.

21. Morrow, *Covenants of the Prophet Muhammad*, 109.

22. Ahmed El-Wakil, "The Prophet's Treaty with the Christians of Najran: An Analytical Study to Determine the Authenticity of the Covenants," *Journal of Islamic Studies* 27, no. 3 (September 2016), 273–354, here 274.

23. College of Islamic Studies, Hamad Bin Khalifa University, "The Covenants of the Prophet Muhammad: Why Documenting Historical Texts Can Help Build Social Harmony," n.d.; https://www.hbku.edu.qa/en/news/build-social-harmony (accessed 5 January 2021).

24. Sidney H. Griffith, *The Bible in Arabic* (Princeton: Princeton University Press, 2013), 11.

25. Ibn Ishaq and Ibn Hisham are largely responsible for the body of knowledge available on Dhu Nuwas. Ibn Hisham's book is an edited version

of a biography of Muhammad written by Ibn Ishaq (d. 767). These two works are complemented by Procopius, a Byzantine historian and the author of the *Persian War* (525), who told the story of the Abyssinian "invasion" of Yemen by Emperor Justinian, who sought control over the Himyarite kingdom.

26. The Abyssinian church mentioned in the reports is said to have been created following the proselytization mission of Theophilus, an Arian, who was appointed by Constantius II, the Byzantine emperor, to serve as the bishop of new churches in Abyssinia and Yemen. Constantius II is said to have visited the church in 340.

27. Alexander A. Vasiliev, *Justin the First: An Introduction to the Epoch of Justinian the Great* (Cambridge, MA: Harvard University Press, 1950), 283–99.

28. Guillaume, *Life of Muhammad*, 21.

29. King, "Some Christian Wall-Mosaics in Pre-Islamic Arabia," 37.

30. Cole, *Muhammad*, 95.

30. Miaphysites hold that Jesus is fully divine and fully human, in one physis. The Miaphysite Christological position opposed the final ruling of the Council of Chalcedon (451). Miaphysitism is the Christological doctrine upheld by the Oriental Orthodox Christians, which include the Armenian Aspotolic Church, the Coptic Orthodox Church of Alexandria, the Ethiopian Orthodox Church, the Eritrean Orthodox Church, the Indian Orthodox Church, and the Syriac Orthodox Church.

6. SYMBOLS AND SOULS

1. Lings, *Muhammad*, 313.

2. The holiest object inside al-Ka'bah is a celestial stone that Lings (*Muhammad*, 3) contends was brought by an angel to Abraham from Abu Qubays, a nearby hill, where it had been preserved ever since it had reached earth.

3. Geoffrey R. D. King, "The Paintings of the Pre-Islamic Ka'ba," *Muqarnas* 21 (2004), 219–29, here 219.

4. Jonathan C. Brown, *Muhammad: A Very Short Introduction* (Oxford: Oxford University Press, 2011), 4.

5. The Chaldeans were an ancient people who lived in Chaldea, a land that

encompassed parts of Asia Minor, Mesopotamia, and Syria between the late tenth/early ninth centuries and the mid-sixth centuries BCE. Chaldea, their country, was an extension of the Babylonian Empire. It is often mentioned in the Old Testament in light of the Jewish people being forced to relocate due to the Chaldeans' expansion. The Chaldeans worshipped up to 5,000 pagan deities. Nannar, the moon god, was chief among them.

6. Baldock, *Essence of Rumi*, 109.

7. Lings, *Muhammad*, 17.

8. David D. Grafton, "The Identity and Witness of Arab Pre-Islamic Arab Christianity: The Arabic Language and the Bible," *HTS Teologiese Studies/Theological Studies* 70, no. 1 (2014), 1–8, here 5.

9. King, "Paintings of the Pre-Islamic Ka'ba," 221.

10. Taymaz Tabrizi, "The Prophet Muhammad Safeguards Jesus and Mary's Icons in the Kaba," Berkeley Institute for Islamic Studies, 9 January 2018; http://www.bliis.org/essay/prophet-muhammad-jesus-marys-icons-kaba/ (accessed 21 January 2021).

11. Ibid.

12. Lings, *Muhammad*, 314.

13. The Ghassanids were an Arab tribe said to have established a Christian kingdom in the Levant sometime in the third century. Other scholars have claimed that the arrival of the Ghassanid Christians in the Levant happened much later, after the Himyarite persecution of the Christians of Najran (and other areas of Yemen) in the sixth century. The Ghassanid territory is believed to have stretched from the northern Hijaz to as far south as Medina.

14. King, "Paintings of the Pre-Islamic Ka'ba," 223.

15. Grafton, "Identity and Witness," 5.

16. Lings, *Muhammad*, 328–9.

17. Ibid., 333.

18. Ibid.

19. Ibid., 329.

20. The Farewell Sermon exists in large part due to the work of Ibn Ishaq, as quoted by Ibn Hisham in *as-Sirah an-Nabawiyyah*, and Al-Tabari in *Tarik*. Muhammad's final speech has been translated many times,

but scholars typically refer to several key translations, including those by Ismail K. Poonawala and Alfred Guillaume. Critics have questioned the textual authenticity of the sermon, but this concern is typically attributed to the sermon being a composite constructed from fragments of Muhammad's sayings. The sermon is not directly addressed in any *hadith* (see Mohammad Omar Farooq, "The Farewell Sermon of Prophet Muhammad: An Analytical Review," *Islam and Civilisational Renewal* 9, no. 3 (2018), 322–42, here 324).

21. Farooq, "The Farewell Sermon", 325–30.

22. Muhammad has been recognized as the world's first anti-racist. According to Ibram X. Kendi, an anti-racist is someone who supports anti-racist policy in their actions, expresses anti-racist ideas, articulates views and beliefs that are anti-racist, and learns about and identifies inequities and disparities that exacerbate racism (see *How to Be an Anti-racist* (New York: One World, 2019)).

23. The Farewell Sermon's emphasis on racial equality also appears to have inspired Al-Hajj Malik El-Shabazz (Malcolm X), the African Muslim proponent of black nationalism during the 1950s and 1960s. After performing the *hajj*, El-Shabazz wrote his "Letter from Mecca," in which he stated: "There were tens of thousands of pilgrims, from all over the world. They were of all colors, from blue-eyed blondes to black-skinned Africans. But we were all participating in the same ritual, displaying a spirit of unity and brotherhood that my experiences in America had led me to believe never could exist between the white and non-white." The *hajj* encouraged El-Shabazz to embrace a similar kind of position on racial equality as Muhammad had advocated for in 632.

24. Morrow, *Covenants of the Prophet Muhammad*, 105.

APPENDIX 3: THE COVENANT OF THE PROPHET MUHAMMAD WITH THE CHRISTIANS OF NAJRAN (630)

1. Muhammad ibn 'Abd Allah, "The Covenant of the Prophet Muhammad with the Christians of Najran," in John Andrew Morrow, ed., *Six Covenants of the Prophet Muhammad with the Christians of His Time: The Primary Documents* (Brooklyn, NY: Angelico Press, 2015), 32–8.

APPENDIX 4: THE FAREWELL SERMON (632)

1. This is Prophet Muhammad's own uncle who became Muslim shortly before the Final Sermon.

BIBLIOGRAPHY

'Abd Allah, Muhammad ibn. "The Covenant of the Prophet Muhammad with the Christians of Najran." In John Andrew Morrow, ed., *Six Covenants of the Prophet Muhammad with the Christians of His Time: The Primary Documents*, 32–8. Brooklyn, NY: Angelico Press, 2015.

Akyol, Mustafa. *The Islamic Jesus: How the King of the Jews Became a Prophet of the Muslims*. New York: St. Martin's Press, 2017.

Aland, Kurt and Barbara Aland. *The Text of the New Testament: An Introduction to the Critical Editions and to the Theory and Practice of Modern Textual Criticism*. Grand Rapids, MI: Eerdmans, 1989.

Armstrong, Karen. *Muhammad: A Biography of the Prophet*. New York: HarperOne, 1993.

——— *Muhammad: A Prophet of Our Time*. New York: HarperCollins, 2006.

Asani, Ali S. "On Pluralism, Intolerance, and the Qur'an." *American Scholar* 71 (2002), 52–60.

Al-Baladhuri, Ahmad Ibn Yahya. *Ansab Al-Ashraf*. Damascus: Dar Al-Yaqza, 1997.

Baldock, John. *The Essence of Rumi*. London: Arcturus, 2006.

Bosworth, Clifford E. "Iran and the Arabs before Islam." In Ehsan Yarshater, ed., *The Cambridge History of Iran*, 593–612. Cambridge: Cambridge University Press, 1983.

Bowersock, Glen Warren. *The Throne of Adulis: Red Sea Wars on the Eve of Islam*. Oxford: Oxford University Press, 2013.

BIBLIOGRAPHY

Brown, Jonathan C. *Muhammad: A Very Short Introduction.* Oxford: Oxford University Press, 2011.

Carlyle, Thomas. "Heroes and Hero Worship." Project Gutenberg https://www.gutenberg.org/files/1091/1091-h/1091-h.htm (accessed 16 March 2021).

Cohen, Andrew J. "What Toleration Is." *Ethics* 115, no. 1 (October 2004), 68–95.

Cole, Juan. "Muhammad and Islamic Peace Studies: Interview with Juan Cole." Informed Consent https://www.juancole.com/2018/08/muhammad-islamic-interview.html (accessed 16 March 2021).

Cole, Juan. *Muhammad: Prophet of Peace amid the Clash of Empires.* New York: Bold Type Books, 2018.

College of Islamic Studies, Hamad Bin Khalifa University. "The Covenants of the Prophet Muhammad: Why Documenting Historical Texts Can Help Build Social Harmony." N.d. https://www.hbku.edu.qa/en/news/build-social-harmony (accessed 5 January 2021).

Considine, Craig. *The Humanity of Muhammad: A Christian View.* Clifton, NJ: Blue Dome Press, 2020.

——— *Islam, Race and Pluralism in the Pakistani Diaspora.* London and New York: Routledge, 2018.

——— "Religious Pluralism and Civic Rights in a 'Muslim Nation': An Analysis of Prophet Muhammad's Covenants with Christians." *Religions* 7, no. 2 (2016), 1–23.

Cragg, Kenneth B. *Christians and Muslims: From History to Healing.* Bloomington, IN: iUniverse Inc., 2011.

Donner, Fred M. *Muhammad and the Believers: At the Origins of Islam.* Cambridge, MA: Harvard University Press, 2010.

Eck, Diana L. "What Is Pluralism?" Harvard Pluralism Project, 2006. http://pluralism.org/what-is-pluralism/ (accessed 21 January 2021).

Ehrman, Bart D. *How Jesus Became God: The Exaltation of a Jewish Preacher from Galilee.* New York: HarperCollins, 2015.

El-Cheikh, Nadia Maria. "Muhammad and Heraclius: A Study in Legitimacy." *Studia Islamica* 89 (1999), 5–21.

El-Shabazz, Al-Hajj (Malcolm X). "The Pilgrimage to Makkah." University of Georgia https://islam.uga.edu/malcomx.html (accessed 16 March 2021).

BIBLIOGRAPHY

El-Wakil, Ahmed. "The Prophet's Treaty with the Christians of Najran: An Analytical Study to Determine the Authenticity of the Covenants." *Journal of Islamic Studies* 27, no. 3 (September 2016), 273–354.

Emon, Anver M. "Religious Minorities and Islamic Law: Accommodation and the Limits of Tolerance." In Anver M. Emon, Mark Ellis, and Benjamin Glahn, eds, *Islamic Law and International Human Rights*, 323–43. Oxford: Oxford University Press, 2012.

Farès, Saba. "Christian Monasticism on the Eve of Islam: Kilwa (Saudi Arabia): New Evidence." *Arabian Archaeology and Epigraphy* 22, no. 2 (2011), 243–52.

Farooq, Mohammad Omar. "The Farewell Sermon of Prophet Muhammad: An Analytical Review." *Islam and Civilisational Renewal* 9, no. 3 (2018), 322–42.

Feiler, Bruce. *Abraham: A Journey to the Heart of Three Faiths.* New York: HarperCollins, 2009.

Finegan, Jack. *The Archeology of World Religions: The Background of Primitivism, Zoroastrianism, Hinduism, Jainism, Buddhism, Confucianism, Taoism, Shinto, Islam, and Sikhism.* Princeton: Princeton University Press, 1952.

Fitzmyer, Joseph A. "The Qumran Scrolls, the Ebionites and Their Literature." *Theological Studies* 16, no. 3 (1955), 335–72.

Forness, Philip Michael. *Preaching Christology in the Roman Near East.* Oxford: Oxford University Press, 2018.

Goddard, Hugh. *A History of Christian–Muslim Relations.* Edinburgh: Edinburgh University Press, 2000.

Grafton, David. D. "The Identity and Witness of Arab Pre-Islamic Arab Christianity: The Arabic Language and the Bible." *HTS Teologiese Studies/Theological Studies* 70, no. 1 (2014), 1–8.

Griffith, Sidney H. *The Bible in Arabic.* Princeton: Princeton University Press, 2013.

——— "The Gospel in Arabic: An Enquiry into Its Appearance in the First Abbasid Century." *Oriens Christianus* 69 (1985), 126–83.

Griffiths, Paul J. *An Apology for Apologetics: A Study in the Logic of Interreligious Dialogue.* Eugene, OR: Wipf and Stock, 2007.

Guillaume, Alfred. *The Life of Muhammad: A Translation of Ishaq's Sirat Rasul Allah.* Oxford: Oxford University Press, 1997.

BIBLIOGRAPHY

Günther, Sebastian. "Muhammad, the Illiterate Prophet: An Islamic Creed in the Qur'an and Qur'anic Exegesis." *Journal of Qur'anic Studies* 4, no. 1. (2002), 1–26.

Häkkinen, Sakari. "Ebionites." In Antti Marjanen and Petri Luomanen, eds, *A Companion to Second-Century Christian Heretics*, 246–78. Leiden: Brill, 2005.

Haldon, John. *Byzantium in the Seventh Century: The Transformation of a Culture*. Cambridge: Cambridge University Press, 1997.

Hall, Stuart. "Ethnicity: Identity and Difference." *Radical America* 13, no. 4 (1991), 9–20.

Hall, Stuart. "Cultural Identity and Diaspora." In Jonathan Rutherford, ed., *Identity: Community, Culture, Difference*, 222–37. London: Lawrence & Wishart, 1990.

Hamidullah, Muhammad. *The First Written Constitution in the World: An Important Document of the Time of the Holy Prophet*. Lahore: Ashraf Printing Press, 1941.

Hasan, Mehdi. "Jesus: The Muslim Prophet." *New Statesman*, December 2009. https://www.newstatesman.com/religion/2009/12/jesus-islam-muslims-prophet (accessed 21 January 2021).

Hassan, Riza. "Modernization, Social Change and Religion: A Case Study of the Islamic Ummah." *Lahore Journal of Policy Studies* 4 (2011), 49–58.

Hoekema, Anthony A. *The Four Major Cults: Christian Science, Jehovah's Witnesses, Mormonism, Seventh-Day Adventism*. Grand Rapids, MI: Wm. B. Eerdmans-Lightning Source, 1989.

Ibn Sa'd, Muhammad. *Al-Tabaqat al-Kubra*. Edited and prefaced by M. 'Abd al-Qadir 'ATa. Beirut: Dar al-Kutub al-'Ilmiyya, 1998.

Ignatieff, Michael. *Blood and Belonging: Journeys into the New Nationalism*. New York: Macmillan, 1995.

Kachouh, Hikmet. *The Arabic Versions of the Gospels: The Manuscripts and Their Families*. Berlin and Boston: De Gruyter, 2012.

Kaegi, Walter E. *Muslim Expansion and Byzantine Collapse in North Africa*. Cambridge: Cambridge University Press, 2010.

Kaltner, John. "Joseph in the Qur'an." Bible Odyssey. https://www.bibleodyssey.org/en/people/related-articles/joseph-in-the-quran (accessed 21 January 2021).

BIBLIOGRAPHY

Karabell, Zachary. *People of the Book: The Forgotten History of Islam and the West*. London: John Murray, 2007.

Kendi, Ibram X. *How to Be an Antiracist*. London: One World, 2019.

Khaldun, Abd Ar Rahman bin Muhammad ibn. *The Muqaddimah*, translated by Franz Rosenthal, https://asadullahali.files.wordpress.com/2012/10/ibn_khaldun-al_muqaddimah.pdf (accessed 15 March 2021).

Khan, Maulana Wahiduddin. *The True Jihad: The Concepts of Peace, Tolerance and Non-violence in Islam*. New Delhi: Goodword, 2008.

King, Geoffrey R.D. "The Paintings of the Pre-Islamic Ka'ba." *Muqarnas* 21 (2004), 219–29.

———— "Some Christian Wall-Mosaics in Pre-Islamic Arabia." *Proceedings of the Seminar for Arabian Studies* 10 (1980), 37–43.

Kruger, Michael J. "Did the Earliest Christians Really Think Jesus Was God? One Important Example." Michaeljkruger.com, 11 December 2014. https://www.michaeljkruger.com/did-the-earliest-christians-really-think-jesus-was-god-one-important-example/ (accessed 21 January 2021).

Landau, Rom. *Islam and the Arabs*. New York: Macmillan, 1959.

Lienhard, Joseph T. "The 'Arian' Controversy: Some Categories Reconsidered." *Theological Studies* 48 (1987), 415–37.

Lings, Martin. *Muhammad: His Life Based on the Earliest Sources*. Rochester, VT: Inner Traditions, 2006.

Mass, Michael. *Readings in Late Antiquity: A Sourcebook*. London and New York: Routledge, 2010.

Migne, Jacques Paul. *Patrologiae Cursus Completus*, edited by Jacques Paul Migne, https://brill.com/view/package/9789004199521 (accessed 16 March 2021).

Morrow, John A. *The Covenants of the Prophet Muhammad with the Christians of the World*. Tacoma: Angelico Press/Sophia Perennis, 2013.

Newman, Albert Henry. *A Manual of Church History (Volume 1: Ancient and Medieval Church History, to A.D. 1517)*. Philadelphia: American Baptist Publication Society, 1900.

Noble, Samuel and Alexander Treiger. "Introduction." In Samuel Nobel and Alexander Treiger, eds, *The Orthodox Church in the Arab World, 700–1700: An Anthology of Sources*, 3–38. DeKalb, IL: Northern Illinois University Press, 2014.

BIBLIOGRAPHY

Osman, Ghada. "Pre-Islamic Arab Converts to Christianity in Mecca and Medina: An Investigation into the Arabic Sources." *Muslim World* 95, no. 1 (2005), 67–80.

Patel, Eboo. *Out of Many Faiths: Religious Diversity and the American Promise.* Princeton: Princeton University Press, 2018.

Peterson, Daniel C. *Muhammad, Prophet of God.* Grand Rapids, MI: William B. Eerdmans Publishing, 2007.

Pickthall, Marmaduke William. *The Life of the Prophet Muhammad: A Brief History.* Beltsville, MD: Amana Publications, 1998.

Pirzada, Muhammad Imdad Hussain. *Bukhari: The Sublime Tradition.* Eaton Hall, Retford: Al-Karam Publications, 2019.

——— *ISIS: State of Ignorance: A Reflection on Islam and Moderation, Extremism and Terrorism, and the Fitnah of ISIS (Daesh).* Eaton Hall, Retford: Al-Karam, 2015.

Pope Francis. "For a Culture of Encounter." *L'Osservatore Romano* 38, no. 23 (September 2016). http://www.vatican.va/content/francesco/en/cotidie/2016/documents/papa-francesco-cotidie_20160913_for-a-culture-of-encounter.html (accessed 21 January 2021).

Porter, Joshua Roy. "Muhammad's Journey to Heaven." *Numen* 21, no. 1 (April 1974), 64–80.

Ul-Qadri, Muhammad Tahir. "The Constitution of Islamic State of Medina: The First Written Constitution of Human History." Constitutionofmedina.com. http://www.constitutionofmadina.com/wp-content/uploads/2012/02/Constitution-of-Madina_Articles.pdf (accessed 21 January 2021).

Ur-Rahim, Muhammad Ata and Ahmad Thomson. *Jesus: Prophet of Islam.* Flushing, NY: Tahrike Tarsile Qur'an, 2003.

Rogerson, Barnaby. *The Prophet Muhammad: A Biography.* Mahwah, NJ: Hidden Spring, 2013.

Rolheiser, Ronald. "How to Be a Practising Mystic." *Catholic Herald,* 2 May 2019. https://catholicherald.co.uk/how-to-be-a-practicing-mystic/ (accessed 21 January 2021).

Safi, Omid. *Memories of Muhammad: Why the Prophet Matters.* New York: HarperOne, 2009.

Servetus, Michael. *The Restoration of Christianity: An English Translation* of *Christianismi Restitutio*, translated by Christopher A. Hoffman and Marian Hillar. Lewiston, NY: Edwin Mellen. 2007.

Siddiqui, Mona. *Christians, Muslims, and Jesus*. New Haven and London: Yale University Press, 2013.

Slomp, Jan. "The Meeting of the Prophet Muhammad with Christians from Najran and the Present Muslim–Christian Dialogue." *Al-Mushir* 18 (1976), 227–34.

Smith, Huston. *Islam: A Concise Introduction*. New York: HarperOne, 1998.

Stoker, Henk G. and Paul Derengowski. "A Discussion about the Version of the Bible Available to Muhammad." *In Die Skriflig/In Luce Verbi* 51, no. 2 (2017). https://indieskriflig.org.za/index.php/skriflig/article/view/2262/4776 (accessed 21 January 2021).

Tabari, Ibn Jarir al-. *Jami' al-Bayan 'an Ta'wil Ay al-Qur'an*. Cairo: Mustafa al-Babi al-Halabi, 1954.

Tabor, James D. *The Jesus Dynasty: The Hidden History of Jesus, His Royal Family and the Birth of Christianity*. New York: Simon & Schuster, 2006.

Tabrizi, Taymaz. "The Prophet Muhammad Safeguards Jesus and Mary's Icons in the Kaba." Berkeley Institute for Islamic Studies, 9 January 2018. http://www.bliis.org/essay/prophet-muhammad-jesus-marys-icons-kaba/ (accessed 21 January 2021).

Talk of the Nation. "Armstrong: 'Muhammad; A Prophet of Our Time.'" National Public Radio, 28 November, 2006. https://www.npr.org/templates/story/story.php?storyId=6549530 (accessed 21 January 2021).

The Apocryphal New Testament. "The Shepherd of Hermas." Philadelphia: Gebbie & Co. Publishers, 197–269.

Tibi, Bassam. *Islam between Culture and Politics*. Houndmills, Basingstoke: Palgrave, 2001.

Ünal, Ali. *The Qur'an with Annotated Interpretation in Modern English*. Clifton, NJ: Tughra Books, 2012.

Unitarian Universalist Association. "Khadijah, First Woman of Islam." UUA.org., n.d., https://www.uua.org/re/tapestry/youth/bridges/workshop14/khadijah (accessed 21 January 2021).

US Supreme Court. "Courtroom Friezes: South and North Walls." Supremecourt.gov. https://www.supremecourt.gov/about/northandsouthwalls.pdf (accessed 21 January 2021).

BIBLIOGRAPHY

Vasiliev, Alexander A. *Justin the First: An Introduction to the Epoch of Justinian the Great*. Cambridge, MA: Harvard University Press, 1950.

Watt, William Montgomery. *Muhammad: Prophet and Statesman*. Oxford: Oxford University Press, 1961.

Wills, Garry. *What the Qur'an Meant and Why It Matters*. New York: Penguin Books, 2017.

———. *What Jesus Meant*. New York: Penguin Books, 2006.

Wise, Robert Todd. "Merely a Line in the Sand: A Model for Christian–Muslim Dialogue." *Reformed Journal*, 1 March 2014. https://reformed-journal.com/merely-a-line-in-the-sand-a-model-for-christian-muslim-dialogue/ (accessed 21 January 2021).

Yildirim, Yetkin. "The Medina Charter: A Historical Case of Conflict Resolution." *Islam and Christian–Muslim Relations* 20, no. 4 (2009), 439–50.

——— "Peace and Conflict Resolution in the Medina Charter." *Peace Review: A Journal of Social Justice* 18 (2006), 109–17.

Zinner, Samuel. *The Gospel of Thomas: In The Light of the Early Jewish, Christian and Islamic Esoteric Trajectories*. London: Matheson Trust, 2011.

INDEX

Note: Page numbers followed by "*n*" refer to notes

177

INDEX

INDEX

INDEX

INDEX

INDEX

INDEX

INDEX

INDEX

INDEX

INDEX

INDEX

INDEX